10/09

Meredith Leyva

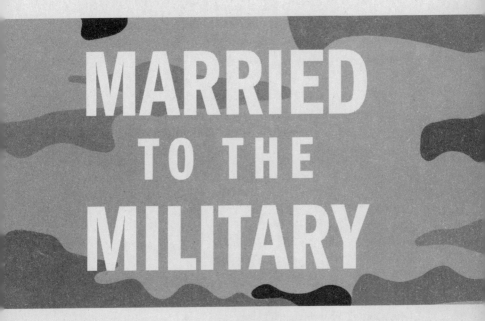

MARRIED TO THE MILITARY

A Survival Guide for Military Wives, Girlfriends, and Women in Uniform

A Fireside Book
Published by Simon & Schuster
New York   London   Toronto   Sydney

FIRESIDE
Rockefeller Center
1230 Avenue of the Americas
New York, NY 10020

Copyright © 2003 by Meredith Leyva
All rights reserved,
including the right of reproduction
in whole or in part in any form.

FIRESIDE and colophon are registered trademarks of Simon & Schuster, Inc.

For information regarding special discounts for bulk purchases,
please contact Simon & Schuster Special Sales at
1-800-456-6798 or business@simonandschuster.com

Designed by William Ruoto

Manufactured in the United States of America

10   9   8   7   6   5   4   3   2

Library of Congress Cataloging-in-Publication Data is available.

ISBN 0-7432-5554-2

CONTENTS

1

Welcome to the Adventure of Military Life!

Welcome to the sisterhood of military women! We are military wives, girlfriends, moms, and women in uniform. Just like you, we had to familiarize ourselves with military life and get to know the community pretty darn quick, sometimes while getting engaged and planning a wedding and other times while reeling from the shock of our Reservist husband suddenly being sent off to war. With all the crazy acronyms, rules, and bureaucracy on top of finding bridesmaids' dresses, it's easy to get overwhelmed—but don't! You can master this, and we are here to help you.

In effect, this book is an orientation manual on military life based on the collective knowledge of military wives and women at *CinC*House.com. *CinC*House.com is a nonprofit organization and community of military women all over the world. In fact, the name "*CinC*House" is military jargon for "Commander *in* Chief of the House." That's what you are! And don't you forget it.

You are the CinC of your house because, while your husband is out playing G.I. Joe, you are primarily responsible for raising the kids, managing the household finances, and establishing yourself and your family in the community. This is no job for the faint of heart. Don't be deceived by the feminine looks of many military wives standing next to their macho men; underneath lies the heart of Scarlett O'Hara. Besides, although the military may joke that "if we wanted a servicemember to have a wife, we would have issued one," your needs and personal and professional goals are just as important as your man's.

Just remember this cardinal rule: Success in military life is all about knowledge and perspective. The purpose of this book is to give you information and a well-rounded perspective on military life so that you can make the right choices for yourself and your family, especially if you are starting a new life as a military wife. This book will:

★ Introduce you to daily life in the military and what you can expect in terms of services and the community—and what is expected of you.
★ Help you understand the benefits and how to get the most out of military life (the business of your marriage).
★ Help you understand and take control of the two primary threats to your sanity: relocation and deployment.
★ Strengthen your marriage by helping you develop a strategy with your servicemember on how to live together.

DEALING WITH JARGON, POLITICAL CORRECTNESS, AND OTHER NONSENSE

Unfortunately, military jargon has become a language all its own. You can refuse to learn it and find yourself corrected or stuck not knowing what was said, or you can become familiar with the basics. We prefer the latter approach, although we limit our use of jargon as much as possible. After all, our hubbies signed up for the job, not us.

To help you through, every time a new acronym is introduced, we write it out fully and explain what it means. We ex-

★★★ WAR STORIES ★★★
Help, I Need to Talk!

I was working 14 hours a day in Washington, DC, at a high-powered corporate public relations agency when my husband first joined the military. Although most of the wives at our command worked, the spouse club was run by stay-at-home moms. That meant most meetings and social events consisted of hours of lunch and bingo or mom 'n' tot play groups.

My girlfriends and I needed more information about military life and what was in store for us. The command was threatening to relocate our families all over the place. Our lives felt completely out of control, and we didn't have a clue how to work the system. However, we also didn't have time to participate in spouse club events and, very frankly, we resented being left out. So did the female servicemembers in our command who wanted to hang out with fellow girlfriends. So we jimmied up a website with a discussion forum that allowed us to talk during the day at work or late at night after the kids went to bed.

Apparently, we weren't the only ones who felt this way, because the website had 40,000 hits in the first month of its existence. By 2003, that little website received nearly 900,000 visitors each month. Thus was the birth of *CinC*House.com.

plain military jargon in the same manner. Chapter 14 is a glossary entitled "Really Stupid Acronyms and Jargon," for your reference. The glossary is also good for translating lingo when on base, especially with the die-hard Marines.

Also, let's skip the political correctness and just acknowledge that this book is written primarily for women, namely military wives and women in uniform. The Department of Defense (DoD) is required to use the term "spouse," but we use the more accurate term "wife." While the number of military husbands has increased slightly, they still represent only 6 percent of all military spouses, and the vast majority previously served in the military and are already very familiar with it. That is very different from a 20-something civilian woman who is just entering or marrying into the military for the first time. We are women, and we want to act and be treated as such.

Additionally, this book takes a fresh approach by recognizing that women in uniform and military wives have common concerns. While military wives are primarily addressed because there are so many of us, many female servicemembers will find it useful because they share the same responsibilities for raising kids and managing households, finances, and relocation. There are plenty of orientation books on military jobs and protocol, but there are almost no good books about handling the family and personal aspects of military life. Thus, the term "military wife" also refers to those female servicemembers who feel married to the military and want solutions to these issues.

Finally, before I get hate mail from nitpickers, let me say that this book covers the general concepts behind key aspects of military life. Different military services, bases, and offices, however, will do things slightly differently. Form 840 on Base A may be referred to as Form 850 on Base B, even though they say the same thing. The two forms are just printed on different-colored paper. What is important is that the concepts are the same, and the book will give you the tools to get through them.

Your husband, boyfriend, or fiancé may freak out when he sees you reading this book. Why on earth, he'll say, do you need to understand this stuff? He'll take care of everything! And he can explain what you do need to know when you need to know it. Right?

Wrong, bucko! You need to know about military life so you can control your family's destiny, and he may not always be around to explain how things work or to handle the situation. Your gut instinct tells you that. What you *can* tell your man is that, by reading this book, you will feel better about entering the adventures of military life, and you will be better able to support him in his mission and have a stronger relationship.

The Least You Need to Know
★ You are neither the first nor the last woman to face the complicated world of military life.
★ This book is designed to help you succeed in taking control of your destiny and strengthening your relationship with your servicemember.
★ The key to controlling your destiny is to learn about military life, including all its acronyms and jargon.

Resources
★ http://www.cinchouse.com—A nonprofit organization and the Internet's largest community of military wives and women in uniform.

2

Your First Day as *CinC*House

GETTING DOCUMENTED

Your first "day" in the military starts with getting proper documentation. If you're a servicemember, you will be walked through most of this, including how to get your family's documentation completed. As a wife, especially one of a Reservist, you need to make sure your servicemember takes care of the following:

★ *Submitting a marriage packet to his command's administration.* No documentation is more important because with it you will be officially recognized and receive the benefits of a spouse by the **Defense Enrollment Eligibility Reporting System (DEERS)**. As a wife, you will be able to shop at the commissary, receive life insurance benefits if your servicemember dies, and obtain health care virtually free of cost. As a girlfriend or fiancée, you get squat. Similarly, a married servicemember receives a substantial increase in pay, but none of it kicks in until the paperwork is submitted.

Military servicemembers receive a substantial increase in pay when they get married! The difference is as little as $100 and as much as several thousands of dollars per month in extra income. But don't make the mistake many couples do and go overboard with family planning. You don't get an extra cent for having kids unless the servicemember is a single parent.

★ *Obtaining a military spouse identification card.* A spouse's military I.D. card obtained from the personnel office looks like a brown driver's license. You will be asked for this I.D. every time you pay for groceries, work out at the base gym, arrive for a doctor's appointment, or go to the bathroom (well, not really). In times of heightened security (referred to as "**threatcon**" or "threat condition"), you will be required to show your I.D. to the guard before entering the base. No I.D., no access without a ton of interrogation and paperwork, even if you live in base housing.

★ *Obtaining a base decal for your car.* A decal from the base security office tells the gate guards and military police that you are allowed to be on base until the expiration date listed on the decal. It also tells them whether the car owner is enlisted or an officer, and officers' cars are typically saluted by the gate guard, even if the spouse is driving. (They're saluting the officer rank indicated on the decal, silly, not you!) Most guard gates require only a decal to allow your car on base. However, if you have an I.D. but no decal, they will hassle you and insist on seeing your car registration, insurance, and other documents stuck to your glove compartment with old gum you left there. Better to be able to whiz through instead of always having to fish out your military I.D. and other documents (car registration and insurance) from the depths of your purse and glove compartment.

★ *Entering you into Tricare.* **Tricare** is the military's very own HMO. Although we address health care in more depth later on, what's important is that you get signed up and assigned a primary care physician so that you have access to virtually free health care at any time, particularly in an emergency. Don't wait for a car accident before you sign up, or you'll be recuperating in a bureaucratic nightmare.

★ *Obtaining a Power of Attorney.* A Power of Attorney, or **POA,** may seem like a big deal, but it's standard equipment for military families. Basically, a POA allows you to conduct business on behalf of your servicemember in his absence, namely during deployments, but it also helps when he's out on training missions and can't be reached. Do not wait for an unanticipated deployment to get your POA. You never know when an event like September 11 will happen and your husband will call you to say he's shipping out in five minutes, see you in six months. Without a POA, you will have no other way to deal with financial institutions, apply for base housing, or do any number of things you never think about when he's around.

Your servicemember may also want to go to the base legal office to write a will. This is a particularly good idea if you have kids or are remarried, but it's not absolutely necessary in the beginning. As with a POA, the process takes an hour or less and is totally free of charge.

Now that you have your to-do list, the first thing you should know is that the official military bureaucracy generally views wives as second-class citizens. That's actually okay. Their first priority should be to care for the servicemembers, who have literally sworn their lives to protecting the United States. (No kidding! Just ask your hubby about his service oath.) Then come the family members, and then come the veterans.

Unfortunately, another reason for this second-class treatment is that other military wives have tried to cheat their husbands by cheating the system, which has forced the military to tighten up regulations, preventing us from doing certain things without the express consent of the servicemember in person or by POA. While there have been only a handful of scams, they've made for great cocktail party stories among the bureaucracy, and most of them pertain to housing, relocation, and pay. Most of them also have to do with a wife milking everything out of her husband before she leaves him.

If you're one of these wives, be forewarned: They know you're coming. And you stink for lousing things up for the rest of us.

The final reason the bureaucracy may treat you badly is because it's just plain tradition to treat women like "little ladies." The good news is that they will call you "ma'am" and open doors for you. The bad news is that you will find your intentions and intelligence being questioned. And you'll find yourself being called a "dependent," which is an old-fashioned but insulting term for what officially is now designated a "family member."

The bottom line is that this second-class treatment can inhibit your ability to get business done on base, and it totally prevents you from obtaining proper documentation without the assistance of your servicemember.

The good news? Your servicemember can do all these things a lot more quickly and efficiently than you can—so just send him! You have enough on your to-do list without adding these mind-numbing tasks to it. However, as you can see, it's absolutely critical you make sure he completes them. In fact, it's worth harassing him a bit to make sure he has completed his tasks.

GETTING TO KNOW YOUR BASE

As you're getting your documentation and running errands on base, take a look around and get to know what services are available to you and where they are located. Some bases are absolutely huge, so get a map at the guard gate and take the time to drive around. Besides finding out where all the great shopping is, you might get to see tanks whizzing by, Cobra helicopters in battle formation, and all kinds of other thrilling stuff that makes for good cocktail party stories.

Every base pretty much has the same services, but smaller

bases have smaller buildings. The **Exchanges** (or military-run department stores) and affiliated specialty stores might become your new hangouts. Each military service has a different name for its department store, but they are all intended to provide savings for military shoppers and basic needs for military families overseas. The Army calls it the **PX** for "Post Exchange"; the Air Force calls it the **BX** for "Base Exchange"; the Marine Corps calls it the **MCX** for "Marine Corps Exchange"; and the Navy and Coast Guard simply call it the "Exchange." Except for the Navy's, all the Exchanges are operated by the Army and Air Force Exchange Service or **AAFES** (pronounced "a-fees"), so you might want to get used to that name, too.

Similarly the **commissary** (the military-run grocery store), which is run by the Defense Commissary Agency, or **DeCa**, effectively subsidizes the cost of food for military families.

Other great family services are provided by the Morale, Welfare, and Recreation (**MWR**) division of the military—sometimes called the Air Force Services Agency (**AFSA**) in that service—including free health clubs with the latest aerobics classes and equipment, free or discounted entertainment and resort tickets from the Information, Tickets & Tours (**ITT**) office, and rentals of outdoor, camping, and party equipment for next to nothing. We've even seen activities like surfing classes, hobby shops, and kids' summer camps organized and promoted by MWR, so be sure that you get a monthly update on what's available by checking your base newspaper.

Speaking of which, your base newspaper can typically be

★★★ **DID YOU KNOW?** ★★★

A military I.D. gives you access to any U.S. military base— Army, Navy, Air Force, Marines, or Coast Guard—with the exception of a few high-security bases.

found outside any major public area on base such as the commissary and Exchange. Sometimes it can also be found online on the official website of your base. It is published weekly by the base **Public Affairs Office,** and contains oodles of information about activities, interest clubs, spouse clubs, and even classified ads. Since there's no cost, you might as well make a habit of picking it up every time you get a chance, to find out what's happening near you.

Finally, you need to know where the family support offices can be found, even if you never expect to need their help. Inevitably, you will need to find them for something at least twice during your stay, and it's usually in an emergency or when you're pressed for time. We'll discuss these services later in more detail, but you should at least be able to locate the following:

★ Personal Property Office (PPO) or Traffic Management Office (TMO)
★ Legal office
★ Hospital or health care clinic
★ Family Support Center
★ Fisher House's emergency child care center
★ Child Development Center (a.k.a. child care)
★ The Navy–Marine Corps Relief Society, Air Force Aid Society, or Army Emergency Relief

While DeCa officially states that it saves military families as much as 30 percent on the cost of groceries, a survey by *CinC*House.com found the savings as high as 44 percent on everyday items! Amazingly, the commissary also makes grocery shopping actually feel luxurious by having baggers available to bag and load your groceries for just a few bucks. And you will never be as happy to see the commissary as when you live overseas and have a hankering for peanut butter.

The Least You Need to Know

★ In order to get the benefits you are entitled to, your servicemember must do five important things: Submit a marriage packet to his command, obtain a military I.D. card for you, put a base decal on your car, enter you in the Tricare system, and grant you a Power of Attorney.

★ The bureaucracy for obtaining these items is irritating, so let your husband take care of it—and nag him like his mother until he follows through.

★ Before your servicemember deploys and leaves you to fend for yourself, take the time to drive around the base and familiarize yourself with the services and resources available to you.

Resources

★ http://www.commissaries.com—Find out the latest specials at your base commissary.

★ http://www.aafes.com and http://www.navyexchange.com— Purchase items from the Exchanges online or find out what's on sale.

3

Controlling Your Family's Destiny

Understanding your hubby's job is not only important for good marital communication, it is also key to coping with the twin obstacles of relocation and deployment. By **relocation,** we mean moving from one city to another, anywhere in the world, so that your hubby can take up a new tour of duty at a new military base. **Deployment** is when the servicemember leaves his family and goes out in the field for patrols, war games, training, and real combat.

Military wives and female servicemembers with families generally try to avoid relocation and deployment because it causes stress on the family. While short absences make the heart grow fonder, long absences can lead to loneliness, guilt, or resentment for being left behind as a single parent. Unfortunately, many servicemembers don't feel the same way about relocation and deployment. As overgrown Boy Scouts, this breed of servicemember loves running around with tanks and artillery in the middle of 104°F Middle Eastern heat for months on end. Plus, this is the main reason why they get paid.

You should expect and respect the fact that, at some point, your servicemember will be deployed and your family will relocate, possibly at the same time. The key is learning to control your destiny to the extent you can by understanding the military system and choosing a strategy that works best for your family. This chapter will teach you about the military system; chapter 10, entitled "Marriage Hoo-ah," will guide you in developing your own family strategy.

GETTING STARTED IN THE MILITARY

With rare exceptions, most servicemembers and Reservists begin their new careers by attending basic training and technical schools if they are enlisted, and Officer Candidate/Training School (**OCS/OTS**), Officer Indoctrination School (**OIS**), Reserve Officer Training Command (**ROTC**), or a service academy (Air Force Academy, the Citadel) as officers. Enlisted servicemembers going through basic training are referred to as "recruits" and are not considered real servicemembers until they pass; officers-to-be are referred to as "officer candidates."

All of these training programs require servicemembers to leave their families for six weeks to six months, and some are more rigorous than others. The most rigorous programs, such as Marine Corps boot camp, have strict rules about what recruits can keep with them, so be sure to get a list of approved items from the boot camp command before your servicemember goes. It can be very embarrassing—and will probably add more physical difficulties to your man's training program—if you send him an unapproved item and he gets caught. You don't want dirty pictures of you passed around the camp, and the instructors or recruits will inevitably find the restricted item and make an example out of your man.

All basic training rules about phone calls, family visits, graduation, and restricted items should be obtained directly from the basic training command, and they will probably arrive in an information packet before the servicemember leaves. Many wives, previously familiar with their man's schedule, get

*The Simplest Thing Can Lead to
Big Trouble at Boot Camp*

After carefully reading the boot camp instructions and talking to other wives, my girlfriend Carrie was determined to send her boyfriend a simple care package that would not get him in trouble. Her care package consisted of homemade cookies (good for buttering up his drill sergeant and fellow recruits) and a few pictures of her with his parents, topped with little sparkles and confetti. Unfortunately, when her boyfriend ripped open the package, the confetti flew everywhere, and little sparkles found their way into every crevice of the wooden floors of his bunk room. As a result, the boyfriend was forced to deep clean the floors—but only after doing un-limited push-ups.

desperate for information about exactly when he can call home and when family can visit. Forget about having that kind of control—seriously. The bottom line is that basic training owns your man until graduation day, which is about the only time you will see him. It's a bit of a shock entering military life this way, but the best thing you can do is let your man focus on passing basic training by giving him praise and encouragement instead of nagging and complaints. If he doesn't pass, he'll have to do it all over again unless he's flat kicked out.

The servicemember's career track is typically determined when he is recruited, and additional training such as tech school is likely required. These are less strict in terms of family interaction, and, again, each training command will give you detailed instructions regarding family interaction. If they don't, ask the command administrator (or "admin") so you don't break any rules but enjoy every opportunity to see each other. This is not basic training, so your hubby should not be embarrassed about asking when it will be appropriate to spend time with family.

Once your hubby passes training, he will be assigned a **detailer,** someone who is responsible for helping him determine his career track and assigning his orders to new billets (i.e., jobs) and locations for the duration of his career.

UNDERSTANDING CAREER TRACKS

One of the most important things you can learn about the military is that the more special skills your servicemember acquires, the more pay and career options he gets. Whether it's aviation mechanics school or college, educational opportunities are some of the truly great benefits in the military, and your family should take advantage of them.

Not only is the education paid for (while he continues to receive a salary), he may get even more pay when he passes and goes to work with his new skills. Further, you can choose career tracks that improve your chances of meeting family goals, such as relocating to specific places (whether it's back home to your family or a coveted spot in Hawaii) or limiting how often your servicemember is required to deploy. For example, Public Affairs personnel are used mainly at base or command headquarters, so they are less likely to deploy and more likely to have a better selection of billets to choose from.

Finally, your husband's choice of career track will ultimately determine the type of job he will qualify for when he decides to leave the military—which he will eventually do, no matter how often he wears his combat boots to bed. The reality is that an infantryman may do all kinds of fun stuff in the field, but in the civilian world he may be qualified only for security jobs such as the local police force or highway patrol. A computer programmer, however, can walk out of the military into a six-figure salary if he plays his cards right.

For these reasons, deciding on a career track is a decision for the whole family, and it's important that you research and discuss the options in partnership with your hubby. Find out what his interests are, search the Web to identify training schools and locations, and, most important, work closely with and ask questions of his detailer. Leaving your hubby's career track to the winds of fortune is asking for trouble. An indecisive hubby will be the first to deploy, the last to return, and the most likely to be stationed in Diego Garcia (if you don't know where that is, use your imagination).

THE DAILY GRIND

Each military job falls under a "command" or department, and each command has its own rules and administration. Most of

★★★ WAR STORIES ★★★
Why Recruiters' Jobs Are Considered Worse Than Deploying Billets

You would think that after years of being deployed to places like Bosnia, Talia's husband would have been thrilled to get a billet as a recruiter near their hometown of Tallahassee. Certainly, their parents were thrilled when they heard the news. But the family quickly learned that recruiters often spend late nights in the office cajoling last-minute walk-ins into joining the Army. Talia couldn't plan a romantic evening or a family dinner because she couldn't count on her hubby to be home. Their parents couldn't understand why he didn't just leave at 5 P.M. Talia's husband stayed at the office because of the tremendous pressure to make the monthly quotas of recruits. And he hated "selling" the Army and feeling the need to be less than forthright about some of the hardships. The couple were thrilled when a billet opened with a supply unit, even though it meant more deployments to Bosnia.

your hubby's paperwork (such as Page 2 of his service record, which enters you officially as a spouse) is submitted through his command admin.

Although the military's hours of operation typically run from 7:30 A.M. to 4:30 P.M., each command may operate on some variation of those hours and require servicemembers to do night watch. Many commands require the servicemembers to get up at o' dark thirty for **PT** (physical training). Obviously, little details like this can make a big difference in a three-year billet, so it's important to check these things out when reviewing billets with the detailer.

Deployment schedules are another critical item. They vary not only from service to service and command to command, but also from billet to billet. And the deployment schedule touted by the command does not always jibe with the real deployment schedule. For example, folks serving on surface ships such as aircraft carriers are supposed to deploy for 6 months and return for 18 months, but these days they are more likely to deploy for 7 to 9 months and have less shore time. Correspondingly, pilots sometimes spend less time on deployment because they can simply fly home when they are no longer needed. So whenever possible, talk to your servicemember's colleagues and supervisors who have had your prospective billet or career track in the past before choosing to accept it. Oftentimes, you can also find the same information from wives on the discussion boards of *CinC*House.com and other Internet sites.

THE REALITY OF RELOCATION

The frequency of relocation and the duration of each assignment are determined by your hubby's career track and specific billet. The average military family relocates every three years, and approximately 80 percent live in the Continental United States

(**CONUS**). Of the 20 percent who live overseas, or **OCONUS**, most live on a variety of bases scattered throughout Western Europe and Japan. Some, however, are assigned to "unaccompanied" billets (i.e., they cannot officially bring their families) in remote locations such as the Demilitarized Zone of South Korea or Guantánamo Bay, Cuba.

Although unaccompanied billets are shorter (typically only one year), the military has begun to recognize the damage these billets can do to a family, chiefly the emotional isolation that can lead to divorce, and whenever possible they are making more accommodations for families in exchange for longer tour durations. You should recognize the possible damage of unaccompanied tours, too. In the experience of *CinC*House, a long absence does not make the heart grow fonder—it makes it resentful of having to be alone and raise children as a single parent. Do not agree to an unaccompanied tour unless there is absolutely no choice. If necessary, look for civilian accommodations to keep you and your family close to your servicemember.

Generally speaking, the military prefers to intersperse popular billets with less-popular billets. The value of billets is determined subjectively by the location as well as the frequency of deployment or hardship. So, for example, a one-year unaccompanied Army supply billet in Afghanistan could be considered as

★★★ **DID YOU KNOW?** ★★★

Servicemembers who request an unaccompanied tour unknowingly send up a red flag to their superiors. Such a request is usually an indication of family problems that the servicemember is trying to avoid. More often than not, the servicemember uses the lengthy separation as an excuse to get a divorce.

bad as an accompanied, nondeploying three-year tour in Korea. By contrast, a billet at Lakenheath Air Force Base (AFB) in England might be considered as terrific as a billet near grandparents in San Antonio, Texas.

Another factor in relocation is that the military tends to relocate families within regions because it is costly to move households across the country or around the world. Thus, West Coast–based families are likely to stay on the West Coast or move to the Pacific Rim (such as Hawaii or Japan), but they are not likely to get billets in Europe. Occasionally, they relocate from the West Coast to the East Coast or vice versa. East Coast–based families are likely to relocate to Europe or the West Coast, but not to the Pacific Rim.

Knowing these factors allows you to take control of your family's destiny by plotting out your goals for future billets. They may seem confusing, so here are some examples:

Sarah and Ben

Sarah works in Washington, DC, where her husband, Ben, is stationed at the Pentagon as a submarine warfare specialist. Although she loves her job, she dreams of living in Europe someday. The couple has also agreed that they want Sarah to stay home when they raise a family, and Ben would like to live close to his parents in Florida and not have to spend too much time away from his growing kids.

Because the couple already lives on the East Coast, and a political desk job at the Pentagon is not considered to be a popular billet compared to being out in the field, Ben is able to work with his detailer to go on an exchange program in London with the British Navy for two years—fulfilling Sarah's dream. Upon return, however, he is required to go to a deploying submarine billet, but he is able to find something in unpopular Kings Bay, Georgia, which is 30 minutes from his parents in Jacksonville, Florida. With his experience in the submarine community, Ben knows that "Boomers" (the big submarines carrying nuclear weapons) deploy for less duration than fast-attack submarines, and he is able to get himself assigned to one. Although Sarah has difficulty finding a job in Kings Bay, the cost of living is very inexpensive and she sees Ben so frequently they can easily start a family while she stays home.

Debbie and Steve

Debbie and Steve live in San Antonio with teenage children. At this stage of their lives, they do not wish to relocate because Debbie is at the top of her career as a corporate executive and they want to keep the children in the same school. Steve is currently an instructor at a tech school, but his detailer says his next billet will be tougher. Steve opts for an aviation billet based in San Antonio, even though it means he deploys frequently for a total of six months per year throughout the three-year duration. After any deployment, he always comes back to home base in San Antonio.

Mindy and Evan

Evan just completed Marine Corps boot camp, but he knows he doesn't want to stay in the military forever, and neither does his fiancée, Mindy. In fact, he was enticed by the educational opportunities touted by the recruiter because he can't afford to go to college. Evan opted to get his technical training at a computer programming center, which happened to be located in San Diego, where Mindy lives with her parents. Although he sometimes gets sent on difficult war games in the California desert for weeks at a time, his growing computer skills make him increasingly invaluable.

Not only does he get the opportunity to remain for a tour of duty at Camp Pendleton in San Diego, he is promoted early, and the additional pay allows him to get married sooner than he expected. Although the admin at Camp Pendleton would like him to stay for a second tour, Evan knows it might mean some (albeit few) deployments. As an alternative, he is considering going to a local university (paid for via the military's Montgomery G.I. Bill scholarship) or getting out and earning a $65,000 salary with a local software company.

RESERVISTS' DUTIES

The typical Reservist drills one weekend out of every month and two weeks in the summertime. But don't get the common mistaken impression that your hubby is just playing G.I. Joe for the weekends only! Your hubby may have the same misconception because he's in it for the extra pay and education benefits. Prepare yourself emotionally, logistically, and financially for the prospect of his being activated and deployed.

Reservist jobs are almost as diverse as those for active duty, so it's just as important to review a career track for potential downsides. In particular, some Reservists such as medical personnel are far more likely to be activated and deployed than others. Ask your servicemember's colleagues about their experiences and what is likely to occur.

DIFFERENCES BETWEEN MILITARY AND CIVILIAN JOBS

As you can see, there are tremendous benefits to a military career, just as there are hurdles to overcome. Comparisons to civilian careers are difficult. Although military servicemembers are paid between 7 and 10 percent less than their civilian counterparts—and wives often have difficulty maintaining an income because of frequent relocations to unusual areas—how many companies do you know that offer free education, amazing benefits, and the opportunity to live in dream locations such as Europe? Your hubby may also like the military because of the excitement. After all, how many cooks or nurses get to brag to their friends about target practice with an M16 or flying in an Apache helicopter? Finally, your kids will appreciate the close-knit community that will greet them anywhere in the world.

Unlike civilian companies, the military will get involved in your personal life, for good or bad. Because the military community lives *and* works together, because military families are de facto diplomats overseas, and because personal issues can affect national security, the military simply has no choice but to acknowledge and regulate the personal lives of its servicemembers.

Spousal and child abuse, for example, can end a servicemember's career, and neighbors *will* call his command to report it—as they should. You don't find that kind of protection in civilian neighborhoods these days! On the downside, extreme personal financial problems can cause your hubby to lose his security clearance because of the increased risk of bribery.

★★★ DID YOU KNOW? ★★★

A revoked security clearance could end a servicemember's career. Yet 60 percent of revoked clearances are caused by personal financial problems! That's because creditors know and frequently do call up a debtor's commanding officer and demand that he pay up. Doing so is technically illegal, but it never fails to work. When the commanding officer hears about a servicemember's mounting debt and his wife's uncontrollable shopping sprees, he will insist the servicemember pay and probably require him to participate in financial counseling. Regardless, the situation immediately sends up a red flag and threatens the servicemember's status. So be sure to pay your bills on time and lay off the trips to the mall!

Finally, the biggest difference between military and civilian life is that the "boss" provides more comprehensive support for the families of the "employee." You will find help around every corner to get you through relocation, career changes, child care, and all kinds of household issues, because the military understands that a servicemember's morale—and therefore his decision to remain in the service—is often determined by the stability of the family supporting him.

The Least You Need to Know

★ If you understand how your servicemember's career track works and what he is destined for, you can better control your family's destiny in terms of your relocations, your job stability, and how frequently he deploys.

★ Basic training kicks off every enlisted servicemember's and Reservist's career. It's a brutal separation, but it's important to let your man get through it without nagging him, so you can move on to better times.

★ Try to learn as much as possible about a career track or command before your servicemember takes a position with it. His colleagues can tell you how much he is likely to relocate and deploy, and give you the unofficial scoop on what life will really be like.

★ You will have to relocate at some point. The key is learning what options you have and working the system to get what's right for you. You and your servicemember will need to discuss your dream and make a ten-year plan.

Resources

★ http://www.staynavy.navy.mil—A career development website for sailors.

★ If you want to do research on career tracks anonymously, check out the official website of your military service or talk to a recruiter. Also, visit Internet discussion groups of servicemembers in career tracks and ask them about their jobs.

4

Community and
Family Resources

GOVERNMENT AND NONPROFIT
ORGANIZATIONS

Just when you thought you had to face military life alone, be assured that help is always available. In fact, there is a wide variety of family support organizations out there, both government-run and nonprofit groups. Their job is to help you cope with the rougher aspects of military life. The government offices in particular know "when mama ain't happy, ain't nobody happy," meaning that an unhappy family will ultimately drive a servicemember out of the military and begin to harm retention levels.

To begin with, there are a number of new-spouse orientation programs offered by a variety of organizations, depending on which base you live. Most Marine Corps bases, for example, offer the highly recommended **L.I.N.K.S.** program through the base chaplain. Whether you're religious or not is irrelevant: L.I.N.K.S. will get you up to speed in a hurry, and you'll find a good friend and counselor in the chaplain. Ask around and check your base newspaper to find out which orientation programs are most helpful.

Occupational licenses, such as nursing, obtained in one state may not be valid in another state. This is particularly true in the People's Republic of California. Check with the career counselor or state occupational safety board website to find out if your occupational license is accepted at your new duty station.

The government-sponsored family support offices can also be a terrific resource. In typical bureaucratic fashion, they are given different names by different services and bases, so it might also be called the Family Services Center or Family Support Center (**FSC**), Fleet & Family Support Center (**FFSC**), Marine Corps Community Services (**MCCS**), or Army Community Services (**ACS**). For practical purposes, this book will simply refer to the Family Support Center or FSC.

FSC on your base is staffed with a dozen or so counselors to assist you in dealing with such critical issues as career resources and training opportunities for spouses, relocation assistance, and personal financial counseling. More recently, career training and job placement have been expanded to include licensing programs. Several military services have also teamed up with job placement agencies to provide spouses with job benefits and training in addition to job placement as the spouse relocates.

Relocation assistance is probably the biggest reason you will use the FSC. The counselor can personally walk you through a move, especially a complicated overseas move, and provide you with brochures and contacts on your new base. This information can also be found on the **SITES** (Standard Installation Topic Exchange Service) website at http://www.dmde.osd. mil/sites.

Equally important, the relocation counselor is your cash

king! He or she can help you determine how much extra money you will receive to cover the cost of the move and whether a "do-it-yourself" (**DITY**) move would be more or less costly than allowing a professional company to handle your move at the military's expense.

FSC is also home to Family Advocacy, the agency responsible for handling domestic violence cases among military families. Family advocates are not perfect human beings, but when contacted promptly with all the information, they do a great job representing abused spouses, often in the face of a servicemember backed by a command full of men. Indeed, it is important to remember that the military is responsible for its employees, i.e., servicemembers, and not their families. The minute some military supervisors begin to see a family break up, they assume the spouse should be cut off from key services, such as access to legal and financial support, in order to protect the interests of the servicemember. Know your rights, girlfriend! Family advocates understand this process, which is reasonable, and know how to work the system on behalf of the spouse. Domestic abuse will also be discussed later, in chapter 13, "Preventing Trouble in Paradise."

Finally, the FSC is home to key financial support services within the Army and Air Force: the Army Emergency Relief and Air Force Aid Society. In the Navy and Marine Corps, these services are provided by a nonprofit organization know as the Navy–Marine Corps Relief Society (NMCRS). *CinC*House could not be more supportive or impressed with these services!

Basically, these organizations provide emergency financial support to military families in need. For example, if a bureaucratic glitch causes your military pay to be delayed, these organizations can immediately advance you the amount if you agree to pay them back upon receipt of the delayed funds. They also provide interest-free loans for things like car repairs, emergency trips home, and some medical services not covered by Tricare. Really extraordinary expenses are covered by grants that do not need to be repaid.

What's the catch? These organizations want you to take responsibility and control of your personal finances, and they will help you do that not only through emergency funding but also through budget counseling. Typically, a financial counselor will start by reviewing your monthly income and expenses and *then* discuss your immediate financial needs. If you don't show responsibility for your personal finances, they won't provide emergency funds—and can you blame them?

In addition to providing emergency funds, these organizations are a terrific resource to help you figure out your household income and expenses in preparation for major changes in your life. For example, it's a great idea to visit a budget counselor when you're anticipating a promotion, relocation, divorce, or new baby. A budget counselor can help you determine *exactly* how much money you will earn and what your expenditures will be so you can be prepared and plan ahead. The NMCRS "Budget for Baby" class is especially famous for its good advice on financial preparations for a new baby as well as guidance on

what items new parents will need and how to get them cheap. Of
course, class participants also appreciate the fantastic "Baby Sea
Bag" full of handmade blankets and other goodies they walk
away with.

Speaking of babies, there are Child Development Centers
located on most bases that give steep discounts on day care.
There's always a long waiting list, but single servicemembers
and dual-military couples get priority. The FSC also offers home
day care certification for military wives who want to open day
care businesses in their homes, so check out that option, too.

Although there are many other family support organizations, one last nonprofit worth mentioning is Fisher House. Its
offices provide discounted and emergency child care for families in crisis, and additional services for those in medical crisis.
Again, find out where your local Fisher House is located on base
because, if you have kids, you will probably need it at least once
during your stay on base—and it will be during a period when
you don't have time to leisurely figure out where it is located.

CIVIL SERVANTS VS. BUREAUCRATS:
HOW TO GET BUSINESS DONE ON BASE

Be forewarned: All of these organizations, both government and nonprofit, can be plagued by bureaucrats. Although the dictionary may not distinguish between a civil servant and a bureaucrat, anyone who has dealt with either will notice an immediate difference. Civil servants are those angels who actually care about providing genuine help to military families. They always go above and beyond the call of duty to make sure you're taken care of. Do not abuse these people by pushing them too hard, or they will turn into bureaucrats. Bureaucrats are employees who couldn't care less about your problems, even if it is their job to care.

Unfortunately, the FSC and other family-related organizations are rife with bureaucrats. FSC positions are relatively easy and well paying—perfect for older employees who are biding their time before retirement. Likewise, these bureaucrats tend to hold senior positions over the younger, more altruistic civil servants.

I raise this issue in order to help you get your business done with these often-difficult people. The favorite word of a bureaucrat is "no." Why? Because "no" is a very powerful word that often forces you to beg for their help. Also, the word "no" prevents them from actually having to work.

The key is to prepare yourself for obstacles in advance, be armed with a pen to fill out countless forms, and always behave calmly and professionally. Never, ever yell or insult a bureaucrat, no matter how obnoxious he may be. If a bureaucrat poses an apparently insurmountable obstacle, you *always* have two options. First, ask him, "Well, so what do you think the solution to this problem is?" This forces him to articulate your options. Never say, "So you don't think I can get this done?" The automatic answer to that question is "no"—and that is not the answer you want.

Your second option is to go through the chain of command to the supervisor. This is really the best option if a bureaucrat is unwilling to help you. However, this will be effective only if you have remained calm and professional throughout your discussion with the bureaucrat. This is where yelling or insulting the bureaucrat really harms you, because no supervisor will want to go near a crazed military wife. But if you've behaved calmly and professionally, the supervisor will feel bad for how poorly you've been treated and will go the extra mile to solve your problem. Better yet, you may be doing everyone a service by effectively notifying the supervisor of your poor treatment by her employees and putting the bureaucrat on report. The next time the bureaucrat deals with a wife or female servicemember, he'll be on his best behavior!

SPOUSE CLUBS AND COMMAND FAMILY SUPPORT GROUPS

If official family support organizations are there to provide you with vital information, spouse clubs and family support groups are there to be your friends and *compadres*. These are women who walk in the same shoes and know what you are going through. They are there for you in the middle of the night when the baby is screaming and your husband is off playing G.I. Joe in a faraway land. Ignore your silly hubby and his friends if they tell you these groups are nothing but gossipy henhouses. They don't know what they're talking about. In fact, this is one area where you are fully authorized as *CinC*House to tell them to shut their traps.

Spouse clubs are typically organizations of military spouses on your base. Usually, there is an enlisted spouse (or wives) club and one for officers' wives, although bases are increasingly integrating their spouse clubs to share mutual interests as well as to increase participation.

In the old days, the spouse clubs were your source for information on where your husband was and what the heck he might be doing, but they would also keep anxious families busy with long luncheons and hours of bingo. Today's spouse clubs increasingly cater to working wives, with evening events and web-based newsletters that can update you at your office. Good clubs also offer child care during meetings. Most important, this is your opportunity to quickly meet other wives who share common interests. Spouse clubs reinforce these friendships by organizing social events for the whole family and opportunities for extensive volunteer work on base. The adage that "friendships are experiences shared" holds true with spouse clubs, and you'll meet lifelong friends whom you'll later visit around the world throughout your military career.

Family support groups, sometimes referred to as command spouse clubs, also socialize frequently, but their primary purpose is to provide information on the status of a deployed command, offer counseling and support to troubled families, and keep families busy and focused on positive things like preparing a spectacular homecoming party for their command. They are run by leaders known as **Ombudsmen** (Navy), **Key Volunteers** (Marine Corps), or just elected representatives of the group. Sometimes these groups are led by the wife of the commanding officer. Whether led by the commanding officer's wife or not, these leaders stay closely connected with the command higher-ups, especially during deployments, and are your connection and hope if something goes terribly wrong with your family.

Perhaps the best thing about family support groups is that,

once again, these are women who walk in your shoes and are going through the same things you are—so go to these meetings! Don't ignore your fellow wives or think you're better than they are for being more independent. You will regret this thinking within one month of your husband's deployment, when you're all alone with no one to talk to.

And spouse clubs and family support groups are fun! The first meeting is always difficult because you are meeting new people, but you'll feel better knowing that they are normal people just like you. By the third meeting, you'll be hooking up with friends for lunch and other activities outside the spouse club.

WHAT ARE OTHER MILITARY WIVES AND FEMALE SERVICEMEMBERS LIKE, ANYWAY?

My first introduction to other military wives occurred when my girlfriend MaryAnn held the first party for our new command. At the time, I was a high-powered public relations executive working in downtown Washington, DC, and I was absolutely certain the other wives would be far beneath me. MaryAnn could not have been nicer, which only reaffirmed my prejudice. She inquired about my work, my hobbies, and whether I had kids, always genuinely interested in what I had to say. She then suggested getting together for lunch with some of the other wives. I reluctantly agreed, but only because she had thrown a heck of a party and I appreciated the opportunity to meet other spouses, half of whom were also working women in interesting jobs.

My second encounter with MaryAnn embarrasses me to this day. After yapping long enough about myself, I finally asked about her adventures in military life and what I could expect. It turned out that MaryAnn, who was married to an F-14 backseater, had lived all over the world. In fact, two days after getting married, she had moved to Tokyo and been left by her deploying husband to find an apartment, a car, a job, and a life. MaryAnn told fascinating stories about escorting her husband's aircraft carrier to port in Thailand in a speedboat full of bikini-clad, whooping wives excited to see their husbands. She has entertained diplomats and foreign military servicemembers in just about all types of occasions all over the world.

The bottom line was that I was greatly mistaken for thinking MaryAnn was some naïve little military wife with nothing else to do. She was simply reaching out to me because she understood the importance of quickly establishing friendships. Life and military billets are too short for the kind of condescension I first showed MaryAnn, and I thank my lucky stars she persisted in making friends because I would have been terribly lonely without her.

MaryAnn is a good example of the friendliness you'll see in other military wives—so don't mistake it as their being naïve or silly. But friendliness is not the only familiar characteristic of military wives. Most military wives are career women. In fact, DoD surveys show that 91 percent of junior enlisted spouses (pay grades E-1–E-5) work and 65 percent of all spouses are employed outside the home, while only 57 percent of civilian women work. As noted before, this is a tremendous change from the old stereotype of the World War II–era wives hanging laundry and pining away for their deployed husbands.

Military families also tend to be young, marry young, and have young children at home. Eighty percent of servicemembers are younger than 35, and they average 25 years old at the birth of their first child. In contrast, only 21 percent of American adults are younger than 35. Thirty-nine percent of children in military families are younger than 6, whereas only 32 percent of civilian families have children at all.

Despite our youth, the typical military family is better educated and more comfortable with technology than the average American. In fact, 92.8 percent of military families report having access to the Internet, compared to only 50 percent of civilians. This can be partly attributed to the fact that the Internet has become the primary way for military families to keep in touch with a deployed servicemember. Also, it is telling that only 5 percent of junior enlisted wives do not have a high school education, and 67 percent have acquired a post-secondary education degree such as a bachelor's degree. In contrast, 20 percent of all Americans have not completed high school and only 24 percent have acquired a bachelor's degree, and just 34 percent of people between the ages of 18 and 24 are enrolled in college.

Finally, the military is one of the most racially diverse institutions in the nation. Approximately 20 percent of servicemembers and their families are African-American, compared to the national average of 12 percent, and 8 percent are Hispanic.

Keep these statistics in mind when you meet other military wives for the first time. Above all, forget the stereotypes. Military wives are smart, educated, career- and family-oriented folks like you. And they're definitely people worth getting to know!

THE CASE FOR GETTING INVOLVED

So you've just moved (again), you've gotten the family settled, and, well, it's lonely. It's time to start building a community around you and your family.

"Where to start?" so many women ask. It's not as easy anymore without the "insta-community" wives used to have available in the form of spouse clubs. Spouse club membership has declined for many reasons, both good and bad.

One of the worst reasons for the decline of spouse clubs these days is that no one wants to be a "joiner." The cultural phenomenon of everyone stressing their independence and self-sufficiency contrasts directly with the need to build communities of people with common interests.

We as military wives and women in uniform need to ask ourselves: Is this a healthy attitude for me and my family, given that we will relocate every three years and given that relocation tops the "most stressful" lists? You not only will benefit personally, but by building a network around yourself, you can help your husband and kids become acquainted with new friends. Everyone knows the benefits of having friends around to support you in difficult times. The question is how to go about it.

Spouse clubs are the most obvious place to begin building a community, because they focus on a common interest: women living on and/or recently moving to a military base. However, there are many other types of organizations that may pique your interest. Consider looking into the following opportunities:

★ Book clubs
★ Philanthropic organizations, such as homeless shelters and educational mentors, or the Navy–Marine Corps Relief Society and other nonprofit organizations on base
★ Fitness clubs or tennis, golf, hiking, biking, and SCUBA diving
★ Women's networking groups like the local women's chamber of commerce or local professional organizations
★ Kids' play groups (Gymboree has classes for babies as young as three months.)
★ Local government recreational offerings, such as writing workshops and art classes
★ Investment and finance clubs
★ Churches or other houses of worship
★ College or continuing education courses

Check your local newspaper, library, or bookstore for notices of upcoming meetings.

What if you go to a meeting and don't like what's going on? All the more reason to get involved! You're probably not the only one who thinks things could be better, and if you don't change things, who will? There are lots of ways to change the direction of family organizations on base. Become a command family leader such as an Ombudsman or Key Volunteer. Volunteer your services at nonprofit organizations like Fisher House or the base thrift store. Or even organize base groups over the Web through support sites like *CinC*House.com.

Finally, remember what it's like to move to a new base. Introduce yourself to new neighbors and support community organizations. Your good deed may come back to help you some day.

The Least You Need to Know

★ There are resources available to help you in every emergency imaginable. The Family Support Center is your first stop.

★ There are two kinds of government employees, civil servants and bureaucrats, but you need to be nice to both and learn how to negotiate in order to get things done.

★ Spouse clubs and family support groups are a terrific way to meet new friends and get through stressful times together, particularly when the command goes on deployment.

★ Getting involved in your community helps you and your family get settled as soon as possible and ease the stress of relocating.

★ Other military wives are just like you! So give them a chance and get to know them.

Resources

★ http://www.dmdc.osd.mil/sites—A critical website to get orientation packets for any military base online. Watch out! This is official propaganda, so you will still need to research the unofficial scoop on any base to find out the bad stuff.

★ http://www.cinchouse.com—Visit the Building Community or base sections for spouse club newsletters and e-mail addresses.

5

Protocol, or How to Get Along in a Hierarchy

RANKS AND PRIVILEGES

Most civilians think the military hierarchy is either cool or totally outdated. Either way, it seems very foreign. Certainly, very few employers these days give promotions according to the number of years of service (as opposed to pure merit) and then incorporate that hierarchy into the social structure.

Because the military is so close-knit, you hang out together as much as you work together. Even in today's world, and despite what others may tell you, socializing is absolutely critical to your servicemember's career—not to mention the fact that it's important for quickly meeting new friends and establishing your family in a community. Servicemembers who mingle and throw parties are seen as good for improving morale among fellow servicemembers and their families. These social butterflies and their wives get to know their superiors and stand out in a crowd at promotion time.

Spouses who support their servicemembers' efforts to socialize are even more of an asset. I'm not talking about the demure Miss Melly, who holds back her opinion; I'm talking about

normal, friendly people getting together for fun and conversation. Command officials often view such spouses as a real asset
in providing friendship and leadership to other families in the
command. This is all very unofficial, of course, and no command is legally permitted to insist that you participate, but this
is one of the great unspoken rules to success in the military.

The military hierarchy does come into play during social occasions. Most important, know that there are rules prohibiting
"fraternization" between officers and enlisted servicemembers
and, to some degree, between junior and senior ranks. The same
rules apply to the ranks of Reservists. What fraternization
means exactly can be up for interpretation, but it basically
means that officers and senior enlisted are supposed to keep a
professional distance from the servicemembers they supervise.
Getting drunk with your subordinates is definitely off-limits, but
other situations are less clear, especially since these rules do not
apply to family members. Can you party hardy at an off-base
neighborhood block party that includes people from different
ranks? If you are close friends with the spouse of someone from
the opposite rank, can you invite her husband over for dinner?
All I can say is that you have to decide on a case-by-case basis.

The consequences of fraternization are also unclear. While

When Socializing Does Not Help His Career

My girlfriend Joleen is normally very active with the family support group of her submarine, but at her last command the spouse group was known for being gossipy troublemakers. Instead of associating herself with the spouse club, she and her friends did their own things to support the boat, including baking goodies for the office to enjoy and making take-out dinner runs for the guys on night duty. As she explains, it's best to use your own judgment as to whether your involvement will help or hurt.

there is no specific punishment we have heard of, we are aware that fraternization can lead to decreased respect and increased resentment in the workplace—and that can harm the career of your servicemember. For example, if you are the wife of a junior enlisted servicemember and become best friends with the commanding officer's wife, other families may think your servicemember's recent promotion was the result of favoritism. Or the commanding officer may feel he has to go out of his way to prevent the appearance of favoritism by *adding* burdensome duties on your servicemember. The worst-case scenario, however, is when enlisted servicemembers become too close to an officer and begin to question or laugh off the officer's authority. There is no room in combat for a democracy, and the hierarchy is there to ensure that orders are swiftly given and acted upon for the safety of the entire unit.

For all these reasons, spouses need to understand what the pecking order is, generally speaking, and what the appropriate protocol is.

WHAT THE UNIFORM MEANS

Whether you know it or not, your servicemember wears his résumé on his chest. Each ribbon, medal, or piece of tin (or lack thereof) synopsizes his service in the military and identifies his rank. When your servicemember sees another servicemember, he initiates or responds to a salute according to the "chest candy" on the other. You do not need to know all the ribbons and ranks—and you will never salute anyone!—but you do need to understand the chain of command and the basic symbols that represent each level.

Please note that there is a difference between a **rank,** such as "captain," and a **pay grade,** ranging from E-1 to E-9 for enlisted, O-1 to O-10 for officers, and W-1 to W-5 for warrant officers. Further, different services have different ranks at different pay grades. Thus, an Army captain is a mid-ranking pay grade of O-3, but a Navy captain is a big-shot O-6!

Following are detailed pictures of rank insignia from the Department of Defense (DoD). Rank insignia are generally seen on the shirt collars or shoulders of the uniform. Although these look complex, all you really need to notice is whether the person is wearing a chevron or "stripes" (meaning he is enlisted), metallic bars (a junior officer or warrant officer), oak-leaf clusters (a mid-level officer), or eagles or stars (a senior officer). Once you visualize these images, you'll notice that some servicemembers have more stripes or bars than others. The more they have, the higher ranking they are. And among bars or oak leaves, silver is higher-ranking than its gold counterpart.

Other uniform items, such as a stripe on the pant leg which identifies most enlisted ranks (except in the Army), can help you navigate the hierarchy. However, the rank insignia is what your servicemember is looking for when he approaches another servicemember and determines whether to initiate a salute to a higher rank or respond to a salute from a lower-ranking servicemember.

Officer Rank Insignia

Source: The *Department of Defense Almanac*

Officer ranks in the United States military consist of commissioned officers and warrant officers. The commissioned ranks are the highest in the military. These officers hold presidential commissions and are confirmed at their ranks by the Senate. Army, Air Force, and Marine Corps officers are called company grade officers in the pay grades of O-1 to O-3, field grade officers in pay grades O-4 to O-6, and general officers in pay grades O-7 and higher. The equivalent officer groupings in the Navy are called junior grade, mid-grade, and flag.

Warrant officers hold warrants from their service secretary and are specialists and experts in certain military technologies or capabilities. The lowest-ranking warrant officers serve under a warrant, but they receive commissions from the president upon promotion to chief warrant officer 2. These commissioned warrant officers are direct representatives of the president of the United States. They derive their authority from the same source as commissioned officers but remain specialists, in contrast to commissioned officers, who are generalists. There are no warrant officers in the Air Force.

Naval officers wear distinctively different rank devices depending upon the uniform they're wearing. The three basic uniforms and rank devices used are: khakis, collar insignia pins; whites, stripes on shoulder boards; and blues, stripes sewn on the lower coat sleeves.

★★★ OFFICERS ★★★

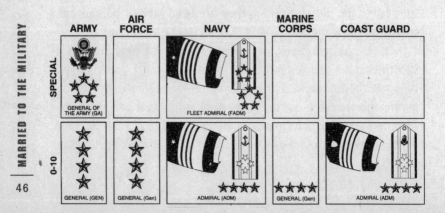

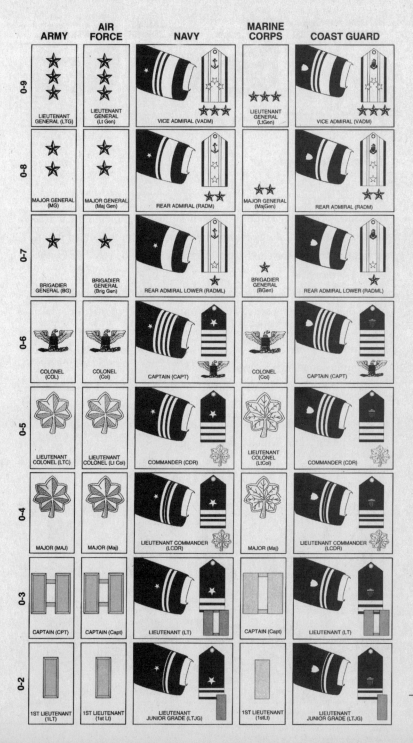

	ARMY	AIR FORCE	NAVY	MARINE CORPS	COAST GUARD
O-9	LIEUTENANT GENERAL (LTG)	LIEUTENANT GENERAL (Lt Gen)	VICE ADMIRAL (VADM)	LIEUTENANT GENERAL (LtGen)	VICE ADMIRAL (VADM)
O-8	MAJOR GENERAL (MG)	MAJOR GENERAL (Maj Gen)	REAR ADMIRAL (RADM)	MAJOR GENERAL (MajGen)	REAR ADMIRAL (RADM)
O-7	BRIGADIER GENERAL (BG)	BRIGADIER GENERAL (Brig Gen)	REAR ADMIRAL LOWER (RADML)	BRIGADIER GENERAL (BGen)	REAR ADMIRAL LOWER (RADML)
O-6	COLONEL (COL)	COLONEL (Col)	CAPTAIN (CAPT)	COLONEL (Col)	CAPTAIN (CAPT)
O-5	LIEUTENANT COLONEL (LTC)	LIEUTENANT COLONEL (Lt Col)	COMMANDER (CDR)	LIEUTENANT COLONEL (LtCol)	COMMANDER (CDR)
O-4	MAJOR (MAJ)	MAJOR (Maj)	LIEUTENANT COMMANDER (LCDR)	MAJOR (Maj)	LIEUTENANT COMMANDER (LCDR)
O-3	CAPTAIN (CPT)	CAPTAIN (Capt)	LIEUTENANT (LT)	CAPTAIN (Capt)	LIEUTENANT (LT)
O-2	1ST LIEUTENANT (1LT)	1ST LIEUTENANT (1st Lt)	LIEUTENANT JUNIOR GRADE (LTJG)	1ST LIEUTENANT (1stLt)	LIEUTENANT JUNIOR GRADE (LTJG)

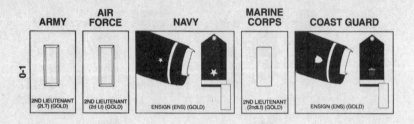

Enlisted Rank Insignia

Servicemembers in pay grades E-1 through E-3 are usually either in some kind of training status or on their initial assignment. The training includes the basic training phase, where recruits are immersed in military culture and values and are taught the core skills required by their service component.

Basic training is followed by a specialized or advanced training phase that provides recruits with a specific area of expertise or concentration. In the Army and Marines, this area is called a military occupational specialty; in the Navy it is known as a rate; and in the Air Force it is simply called an Air Force specialty.

The U.S. Coast Guard is a part of the Department of Transportation in peacetime and the Navy in times of war. Coast Guard rank insignia are the same as those for the Navy except for color and the seaman recruit rank, which has one stripe.

★★★ ENLISTED ★★★

ARMY	AIR FORCE	NAVY	MARINE CORPS	COAST GUARD	
1ST SERGEANT (1SG) / MASTER SGT (MSG)	SR MASTER SERGEANT (SMSgt) / SR. MASTER SERGEANT W/DIAMOND (E-8)	SR CHIEF PETTY OFFICER (SCPO)	1ST SERGEANT (1stSgt) / MASTER SGT (MSgt)	SR CHIEF PETTY OFFICER (SCPO)	E-8
SERGEANT FIRST CLASS (SFC)	MASTER SERGEANT (MSgt) / MASTER SERGEANT W/ DIAMOND	CHIEF PETTY OFFICER (CPO)	GUNNERY SERGEANT (GySgt)	CHIEF PETTY OFFICER (CPO)	E-7
STAFF SERGEANT (SSG)	TECH SERGEANT E-6 (TSgt)	PETTY OFFICER 1ST CLASS (PO1)	STAFF SERGEANT (SSgt)	PETTY OFFICER 1ST CLASS (PO1)	E-6
SERGEANT (SGT)	STAFF SERGEANT E-5 (SSgt)	PETTY OFFICER 2ND CLASS (PO2)	SERGEANT (Sgt)	PETTY OFFICER 2ND CLASS (PO2)	E-5
CORPORAL (CPL) / SPECIALIST (SPC)	SENIOR AIRMAN E-4 (SrA)	PETTY OFFICER 3RD CLASS (PO3)	CORPORAL (Cpl)	PETTY OFFICER 3RD CLASS (PO3)	E-4
PRIVATE FIRST CLASS (PFC)	AIRMAN 1ST CLASS E-3 (A1C)	SEAMAN (SN)	LANCE CORPORAL (Lcpl)	SEAMAN (SN)	E-3
PRIVATE E-2 (PV2)	AIRMAN E-2 (AMN)	SEAMAN APPRENTICE (SA)	PRIVATE 1ST CLASS (PFC)	SEAMAN\ APPRENTICE (SA)	E-2
PRIVATE E-1 (PV1) NO INSIGNIA	AIRMAN BASIC E-1 (AB) NO INSIGNIA	SEAMAN RECRUIT (SR)	PRIVATE (Pvt) NO INSIGNIA	SEAMAN RECRUIT (SR)	E-1

49

★★★ WARRANT ★★★

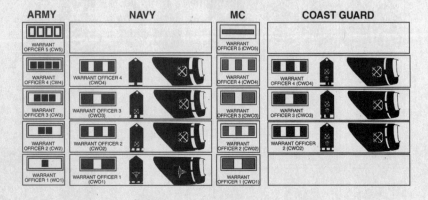

Leadership responsibility significantly increases in the mid-level enlisted ranks. This responsibility is given formal recognition by use of the terms "noncommissioned officer" and "petty officer." An Army sergeant, an Air Force staff sergeant, and a Marine corporal are considered NCO ranks. The Navy NCO equivalent, petty officer, is achieved at the rank of petty officer third class.

AND YOUR NAME IS . . . ?

Once you figure out the rank, you've solved one of the great battles of etiquette on the face of the planet: remembering the names of people you've been introduced to. Let me explain.

Let's say you are introduced to a Captain Ernie Buckforth. Thereafter, you would normally refer to him as "Captain Buckforth" or just plain "Captain." However, because most servicemembers prefer that civilians call them by their first names during social occasions, Captain Buckforth will probably ask you to call him "Ernie." Thus, if you ever forget his name, simply greet him as "Captain"—which is signified on his rank—and wait for him to say, "Oh please, call me Ernie."

You won't have as much luck with spouses, and really polite spouses can actually pose an etiquette problem, albeit a good one. My girlfriend Rose, for example, is the 30-year wife of the Command Master Chief (CMC) on a prominent aircraft carrier. That means her husband supervises all of 5,000 enlisted personnel on board, and he reports directly to the executive officer and commanding officer on their status. Rose, in her position, effectively takes leadership of the enlisted families whether or not she gets actively involved in the family support group. Even so, Rose frequently allows younger, more enthusiastic wives to run the family support group so she can play more of a background role.

The trouble with women like Rose is that they'll never introduce themselves as "Rose, wife of the CMC"—no decent and polite spouse would. She simply introduces herself as "Rose." Those spouses who know the CMC's last name might make the connection, but most spouses don't, and they go on to complain about the status of the enlisted on the ship. Rose says she likes to hear background info that she would not otherwise be told, but she has also heard several obnoxious spouses reveal highly sensitive information in undiplomatic terms (to say the least!). When Rose passes on the information to her husband, the spouse and her servicemember aren't even aware that her unprofessional approach to complaining or revelation of sensitive information is being reported directly to the CMC!

The lesson here is to always behave professionally with other spouses and servicemembers, because you never know who you're really talking to. Equally important, be polite about introducing yourself. Rose is the first to say that she did not earn her husband's rank—he did! So why would she introduce herself as the CMC's wife? And she doesn't want to have friends who are using her to advance their servicemembers' careers.

WHAT TO WEAR? THE APPROPRIATE DRESS
FOR EVERY MILITARY OCCASION

You will be invited to any number of different social events related to the military. These events are a blast if for no other reason than to see the military in its finest dress (you know you love those men in uniform!). Few lucky Army wives leave a "dining out" without being impressed by the Cavalry officers in traditional Stetson hats and riding boots. And those Navy whites will make you as giddy as you were the first time you watched Tom Cruise in *Top Gun*.

The most formal events include the annual service ball (such as the Army Birthday Ball) and diplomatic receptions, both of which can require formal ball gowns for spouses. The

★★★ WAR STORIES ★★★
Not AT&T?

My girlfriend Belle tells a painful story about attending a very traditional tea hosted by the wife of a high-ranking Marine officer. As she walked in, the old dame held out a silver tray to a nervous young woman in front of Belle and asked for her calling card. The guest pulled out her AT&T card in front of the horrified hostess. Belle had to explain the faux pas: The hostess was expecting an old-fashioned calling card, which looks like a business card and provides her with your name so that she will know you attended, even if she does not get the chance to speak with you. Calling cards also allow hostesses to double-check your name and write thank-you notes if appropriate. Very few military wives these days use calling cards, but if you are asked for one, simply say that you have run out of them and not had a chance to go to the printer.

A favorite activity of spouse clubs is to hold fashion shows in preparation for the service birthday ball. Club members parade the latest evening wear, meaning you get a sneak preview of what everyone else will be wearing at the ball. They will also tell you where the dress was purchased and whether the retailer is offering a discount to military wives.

birthday balls are such a big occasion that groups of couples often rent hotel rooms for the night at the location of the event. Examples of slightly less formal events include a traditional "dining out," which is a command-sponsored dinner and dance party that includes spouses and girlfriends, and a Change of Command ceremony, which formally attaches and detaches command leadership to your unit. Finally, you will be invited to casual events such as command-sponsored picnics.

Military uniforms are confusing enough without your trying to figure out the appropriate dress to wear when accompanying your servicemember. After all, the goal is to help your servicemember impress his colleagues and superiors with your classy clothes and good looks. Although trashy fashions are all the rage, anything that says "tramp" will make you a source of gossip.

The first step is to check the invitation to see what is indicated or ask your man what he is wearing. If the invitation doesn't say, ask the hostess what she is wearing. On the following pages is a guide to help you through the quagmire.

Event	Military Dress	Do	Don't
Formal Ball	Army: Dress Blues or Dress Mess; Class A uniforms may be appropriate if you do not have Dress Blues.	Formal gown or tuxedo. Be Cinderella for the evening!	Anything casual or so low-cut that your breasts fall out when you dance. Don't make yourself the subject of gossip at the watercooler on Monday.
	Navy: Mess Dress; whites or blues, depending on the season		
	Air Force: Mess Dress		
	Marines: Dress Blue Bravos (with medals), Dress Blue Alphas (with ribbons and badges), or Service Alphas (green uniform)		
Dining Out or Mess Night (a command-sponsored dinner with spouses)	Army: Dress Blues or Mess; Class A uniforms may be appropriate if you do not have Dress Blues.	Fancy cocktail dress or short formal gown; tuxedo or dark suit and tie for men	The suit you wore at the office that day or anything trashy enough to wear at a nightclub. "Church" dresses are also too innocent for the kind of fun you will have!
	Navy: Dress Blues (winter) or formal "choker" whites (summer)		
	Air Force: Service Dress or Mess Dress		
	Marines: Dress Blue Bravos (with medals), Dress Blue Alphas (with ribbons and badges), or Service Alphas (green uniform)		

Event			
Change of Command, Hail and Farewell Party	Army: Battle Dress Uniforms (BDUs) or "Duty Uniform" Navy: Service Dress Blues (winter) or formal "choker" whites (summer) Air Force: Fatigues or blues (uniform of the day) Marines: Dress Blue Deltas (brown shirt, blue pants) or Service Charlies (green pants, brown shirt)	Evening: Evening dress—but no sequins. This is not the Academy Awards. Dark suit and tie for men. Daytime: Floral dress or business suit unless the party is casual. Definitely ask the hostess.	Casual outfits, including jeans and bare midriffs, or anything your mother would not approve of.
Dinner at CO's House (or equivalent)	Ask the hostess. Usually civilian clothes: oxford shirt and slacks. Tie and jacket may be required.	"Church clothes," such as floral dresses, nice slacks. Something you'd wear to a nice dinner with the in-laws.	Jeans or overly casual clothes (unless the hostess says okay); no bare midriffs or nose rings. Look responsible!
Command-Sponsored Picnic or Potluck	Civilian clothes (polo shirt and shorts)	Nice shorts and tennis shoes. If you expect to swim, limit your bathing suit exposure and bring a cover-up.	Miniskirts or other clothes that will inhibit your ability to play sports; absolutely no thong bikinis! This is not Spring Break!
Spouse Meetings		Khaki pants and a casual top	If your mother would not approve, neither will the CO's wife.

Socializing is a critical function of a spouse, even in the modern world. So get out there and have fun! Don't worry too much about protocol; it's far more important to be friendly and inviting. Not only are you helping your spouse's career, but you may meet a few new friends.

The Least You Need to Know

★ Expect to socialize with your servicemember's colleagues. Not only is it a great way to meet new friends, you're helping him advance in his career.

★ Be aware that officers and enlisted personnel are not allowed to "fraternize" with each other. They are required to keep a professional distance. This rule does not apply to family members.

★ You can learn to distinguish who is who on base by learning more about rank insignia—the "chest candy" on your servicemember's shirt that spells out his rank and résumé.

★ Dress appropriately for every occasion. Most important, don't dress like a tramp, or you will become the subject of watercooler gossip at your servicemember's office.

Resources

★ http://www.defenselink.mil/pubs/almanac/—The Department of Defense Almanac can explain in more detail the military hierarchy.

6

Your Portable Career

As mentioned earlier, military wives and female service-members are no longer the World War II–era sweethearts pining away at home. We are predominantly working women with goals and ambitions that extend way beyond taking care of our husbands. This is an important concept to understand because so many women underestimate the power their careers have in their lives. It's true that many spouses work to make ends meet, in part because the average servicemember earns about 7 percent less than his civilian counterpart. More important, however, career aspirations can be critical to the self-esteem of women today.

The working world cannot fulfill every emotional need of human beings, but there is no denying that some people need that daily sense of accomplishment and financial reward that only a career can provide. Military wives and female service-members often do themselves an injustice by subordinating their professional needs and aspirations to the needs and desires of their husband and family. I'm not suggesting that all women should work; I just want you to be honest with yourself and find a balance that works for you and your family. Just remember, when mama ain't happy, ain't nobody happy. So don't deprive yourself of emotional fulfillment from a career if you really need it. You'll be depriving your family of a happy wife and mother.

I often see wives and female servicemembers rob themselves of career fulfillment by accepting less-challenging positions or quitting work altogether. The frequent relocation of military families, averaging one move every three years, adds to the burden of maintaining a spouse's career and is typically the excuse for blowing off career aspirations. A recent study by RAND, a prominent think tank, found that military wives earn as much as 60 percent less than their civilian counterparts, even though we tend to have higher education levels. Army and Air Force wives tend to fare worse than their Navy and Marine Corps counterparts. Why?

The answer lies in the frequency and place of relocation. In other words, it is difficult to maintain a career track when moving from Oklahoma City to Fort Benning, Georgia, to Japan in three-year stints. Navy wives have the easiest time because so many bases are located in large port cities that offer significant job opportunities. For the other services, however, not only is it difficult to find a comparable job with comparable pay and skills, but spouses have the added burden of facing discrimination from employers who are tired of hiring employees who seem to relocate every time the wind changes. Further, many licensed professionals face the challenges of meeting different state standards, particularly California's, and having to reapply for a license every time they relocate. Finally, there is the issue of time and effort involved in quitting and finding a new job, often over long distances. Thus, many spouses opt for low-paying, unchallenging positions or simply stop working altogether.

Do not despair! Your girlfriends at *CinC*House have several alternatives for those who want to continue their careers.

The most important thing you can do is talk with your servicemember about how you feel about your career, and make sure that he views your professional aspirations as equal to his own. Many servicemembers have a tough time with this discussion because they feel like the spouse is attacking his job in the military, so reassure him that you understand you may have to relocate with his job. In return, he simply needs to be supportive of your career goals and assist you emotionally and logistically with those inevitable career transitions whenever possible. When you relocate, moving duties should be shared equally so that both of you can make your respective career transitions. Do not agree to handle moving duties instead of pursuing career goals just because hubby wants to check in early!

During this discussion with your servicemember, and on your own time, begin to develop a strategy for your own career track. This strategy should cover a long period of time, not only your servicemember's commitment to military service but his transition to the civilian world. It should also take into account your family planning goals.

Your first strategy is to identify a career track that is "portable." You want to be able to take your job skills from base

---

★★★ WAR STORIES ★★★
Online Networking with Fellow Wives

When Heather, who was stationed in Germany, found out her family had orders to move to California, she immediately jumped on the *CinC*House.com discussion boards to find out about her new base and meet new friends. In the process, she met another wife, Lisa, who was also a health care professional and learned that her license was not accepted by the state of California. But instead of suggesting Heather reapply and take a licensing test, Lisa recommended that Heather apply for a job at the base hospital where she worked, since military health care facilities accept all state licenses. Before she had packed her bags in Germany, Heather had filled out an application and scheduled an interview.

to base and quickly find a job. Accounting is a terrific example of a portable career because every military community needs accountants and there are a minimum of licensing hassles. Retail sales, hairdressing, and health care professions (to some extent) are also good choices.

Second, identify national and international companies that need your job skills and would be willing to relocate your job (and benefits) with you. Defense contractors, such as Boeing, Raytheon, and General Dynamics, have offices on or nearby most American military bases in the world. Public relations agencies, management consulting firms, and accounting firms also have offices worldwide. In fact, my girlfriend Kendra has worked for almost three years for a Boston-based public relations agency from her home near Marine Corps Base Miramar in San Diego. The agency paid to equip her home office, and they couldn't be more pleased to add a "San Diego headquarters" address to their letterhead. Kendra loves her career progress and the flexibility of working from home.

The federal government is the ultimate portable employer. Every military base employs a small contingent of government employees to fulfill the basic needs of that community. The very services you've read about in this book, plus all kind of jobs in quality control, secretarial pools, and management, are filled by qualified applicants like yourself—many of them military wives. The trick to government employment is just getting in the door. Completing the civil service application is no small feat. However, if you find a government office that really wants to hire you, it will help you with the paperwork. And once you're in the civil service, you're in! You'll have a leg up on government jobs everywhere.

If your ambitions are larger than what is described here, I strongly encourage you to join a burgeoning new line of spouse entrepreneurs. These amazing women have opened their own lucrative businesses in a portable field of their choice and simply move the business from place to place. Is it risky? Yes, but it can also be substantially more lucrative than if you were to stay in

★★★ DID YOU KNOW? ★★★

Elaine Neetz, employment readiness counselor at the FSC at Fort Wainwright, Alaska, writes:

When families determine that they are going to be relocating, working spouses looking for a job in the civil service should carry the following information with them to ensure that job hunting at the new location goes smoothly and employment is quicker and easier (depending on the job market, of course):

- Updated résumé and/or federal application (SF-171, OF-612, and the Resumix résumé)
- Professional certificates
- School transcripts
- At least three references (addresses, telephone numbers, points of contact)
- Awards, honors, letters of recommendation/appreciation, volunteer portfolio
- Federal employees should have Form SF-50 and Performance Appraisal or Form DD-214, if applying for the first time
- Recent work history
- Civilian employees should call their Civilian Personnel Office (CPO) for information about priority placement/extended leave without pay.

Most bases list their positions on their websites (e.g., http://www.eielson.af.mil/cpo for Eielson AFB, Alaska) with all the qualifying information that needs to be included. Spouses should consult with their local Family Support Center to inquire about the employment expert in their facility. This person should be able to assist any spouse in constructing the résumé to include all required CPO information. This information is usually located on the CPO page at the installation's website.

Your Portable Career

Cutting-Edge Hairstyling in the Rural Florida Panhandle

My girlfriend Marie was trained as a hairstylist in the top salons of Miami Beach. When she had kids and relocated to the Florida Panhandle, she saw it as the perfect opportunity to leave the office politics of the salon and open one in her own home. Because I knew Marie as a friend, I was reluctant to ask her to cut my hair, even though all the wives were her clients. After three months of bad haircuts and juggling a newborn baby, I finally decided to call Marie and schedule an appointment. I quickly learned why she had established such a great clientele through word of mouth and was regularly booked solid.

one place. And instead of job security, you get the benefit of never having to work for another incompetent boss again!

The new generation of spouse entrepreneurs is creative beyond measure. While the military community has always had its share of profitable Avon ladies, Pampered Chefs, and Tupperware parties, the women of this new breed are running their own businesses in personal accounting, hairdressing, cleaning services, day care, freelance journalism, and marketing and public relations. Oftentimes, they gained their experience from a previous employer, discovered they could run their own business better, and opened up shop from their home at half the rates their former employer was charging. With a bit of marketing, new clients come around. Better yet, with today's technology, many businesses can maintain current clients by communicating via the Internet, phone, and fax machine while moving from location to location.

So there are a multitude of options for keeping your career alive and thriving, including many family-friendly opportunities.

★★★ **WAR STORIES** ★★★
Road Warrior

My girlfriend Victoria is the ultimate independent virtual assistant. In her pajamas, and in the luxury of her own home, she provides secretarial support services to several business-people located all over the country. When she and her husband relocated to Alaska, she continued her work on the road by simply plugging in her laptop at rest stops. She says that her clients don't mind her family's frequent relocations because they don't see it and it never affects them. All they care about is the excellent assistance she provides, and they pay her well for it, too.

Again, the emphasis should be on what makes *you* happy by fulfilling your professional and financial aspirations. Time and again, I've heard wives complain that their hubby's military career destroyed their career. Bullfeathers! Yes, it is more difficult to maintain a career. In the end, however, those wives allowed their own careers to fall to pieces, and their sense of self-esteem with it.

The Least You Need to Know
★ You can maintain a career while relocating around the world! It just takes savvy and planning!
★ Don't underestimate the importance of your career to your self-esteem, or treat it as less important than your service-member's career. If your job satisfies you, don't rob yourself of happiness by putting your career track last. You'll make yourself and your family miserable.
★ Most career-oriented military wives follow one of three paths: Hone their job skills to a portable career track; work for defense contractors or the government so they can simply transfer when relocating; or start their own business.

Your Portable Career

Resources

★ http://www.usajobs.opm.gov/—USAJOBS is the federal government's official one-stop source for federal jobs and employment information. Includes application forms for downloading.

★ Visit your base website for local job listings.

★ http://www.wahm.com—An online magazine with job boards for work-at-home moms.

7

Personal Finances—
Military Style

HOW MILITARY PAY WORKS

Military servicemembers get a paycheck every two weeks, just like the rest of the world. However, it's important to be aware that the amount paid can vary from paycheck to paycheck. Reservists, too, can see their pay vary substantially. To understand why and how to maximize your servicemember's income potential, you need to understand the components of military pay. Please note that any dollar amounts listed below are 2003 rates.

★ *Basic Pay.* This is the primary source of your servicemember's income and is based on his pay grade (e.g., E-3 or O-1). Congress has increased Basic Pay by approximately 4 percent each year in recent years, although when the military is less politically popular, pay increases may hover around 2 percent. Historically, any increase in Basic Pay goes into effect on January 1. All Basic Pay is taxable income, and the amount of years in service or a promotion increase this pay. Marriage or your husband's service record does not affect it.

★ *Basic Allowance for Housing (BAH, or BHA).* BAH is what the military pays those on active duty to maintain their living quarters, including (allegedly) your utilities. You receive BAH only if you live in civilian housing; you do not receive BAH if you live in base housing. Your BAH is primarily determined by the cost of living in your area, so major cities and overseas locations typically have higher BAH rates than rural areas. BAH is also adjusted by pay grade and according to whether the servicemember is permitted to live off base or has a family or is married—but don't necessarily expect a big jump! In some cases, the difference between BAH with dependents and BAH without dependents can be as little as $50 to $100 per month. BAH is not taxable income.

★ *Basic Allowance for Subsistence (BAS).* This is what the military pays for feeding the servicemember—not for feeding the entire family. That is an important distinction because, although BAS increases somewhat when a servicemember does not have a meal card at the chow hall, it is nearly all docked when he deploys since the military is now feeding him. BAS is the top reason families get into financial trouble when the servicemember deploys, because they don't anticipate the $100 to $200 reduction in monthly pay. BAS is a flat rate for both officers ($167 per month in 2003) and enlisted ($243 per month) and is not taxable income.

★ *Hardship Duty Pay.* This is a bonus of between $50 and $150 per month for serving in difficult areas, either on deployment or in remote locations (for example, an unaccompanied tour to Korea). This income was recently declared nontaxable by Congress.

★ *Hazardous Duty and Imminent Danger/Hostile Fire Pay.* This is exactly what you think it is. When your servicemember faces a dangerous situation, he gets $150 per month for it. This income was recently declared nontaxable.

★ *Family Separation Allowance (FSA).* If your servicemember is away from home consistently for 30 days or more, you are entitled to $100 per month in FSA.

Once you understand the fundamentals of pay, you get into areas of specialty pays, all of which depend on the job skills and job situation of your servicemember. Bottom line: The more training he has and the more difficult the circumstances are, the more he is paid.

★ *Career Sea Pay.* Anywhere from $100 to $600 per month in extra pay is given to sailors and Marines attached to a ship (even in port) for more than 30 days. Increases in sea pay are based on pay grade as well as accrued years of sea duty, and the income is taxable.

★ *Aviation, Submarine, and Other Special Incentive Pays.* This is how the military increases compensation for learning a critical skill. Monitor these pays carefully because your service-member's job choices greatly affect how much Special Pay you receive. Submarine Pay, for example, is among the highest, at an extra $75 to $425 per month. Increases in Special Incentive Pays are based on pay grade as well as years in service. This pay is taxable.

★ *Special Duty Pay.* This is pay designated by the Secretary of Defense for duties considered to be extremely difficult or in-volving an unusual degree of responsibility. Although this pay is geared more toward drill instructors and recruiters, in wartime it applies to many deployed servicemembers. Usually $100 or more per month, this pay is taxable.

★ *Overseas and CONUS Cost-of-Living Allowance (COLA).* You can get big bucks for living overseas or in Alaska and

Hawaii, especially in less popular or high-cost places such as Japan. The Overseas COLA is also adjusted by pay grade, and it is not taxable.

Other pays include:

★ *Dislocation Allowance (DLA).* Worth up to several thousand dollars, DLA is *absolutely critical* in helping you cover the cost of relocating your family to a new permanent duty station. Given that the average military family loses $800 per move, it's important you know how much DLA you'll be receiving so you can budget and plan for your trip. This is one to nag your hubby about. This income cannot be taxed.

★ *Per Diem Pay for Temporary Duty (TDY).* If your servicemember goes on a business trip or is asked to do "temporary duty" more than 50 miles from home, he is not expected to pay the cost out of pocket. Instead, he will be given Per Diem pay, which is a daily money allowance to cover the cost of housing and food while he is away from home. As such, this income is nontaxable. Make sure your servicemember arranges for Per Diem pay and saves whatever receipts necessary in order to have his expenses reimbursed. You don't want to pay for his trip on your credit card and have it accumulating interest while the bean counters take their sweet time figuring out how much to pay you back.

★ *Reenlistment Bonus and Other Retention Bonuses.* This requires some negotiation with your detailer, but active duty can earn up to tens of thousands of dollars just for reenlistment. Enlisted reserves earn $750 for a three-year enlistment or reenlistment, and $1,500 for a six-year gig, which is paid in increments over the duration of the enlistment. Be sure to find out what your husband's colleagues have negotiated before you begin discussions with the detailer, or you may be missing out. There may be extra bucks for servicemembers with critically needed skills as

The government issues traveling servicemembers a credit card and asks that they charge all travel-related expenses on it. Watch out! You must pay off the *entire* amount of your bill—even if you have not been reimbursed—or you get reported to your command and may be prosecuted! Servicemembers on six weeks temporary duty often get screwed because the statement arrives at their home while they are away and they don't have the opportunity to pay it. Simply put, you are not permitted to accumulate debt on your card. Also, you are not allowed to use the credit card for personal items, so don't even think about buying that new television on government credit.

an incentive to stay in the service. Also, please note that your bonus is taxable, so don't spend it all.

★ *Uniform Allowance.* This once-per-year nontaxable stipend for enlisted covers the cost of uniforms and other mandatory purchases related to your servicemember's job. The amount ranges between $200 and $400, and those in special units such as the Army Band get extra money. Officers get this allowance only at the beginning of their career and are expected to maintain the cost of their uniforms out of their own pockets. Warning: Do not spend this money on anything but uniform items! You will end up spending every cent of this pay ensuring your servicemember is properly attired so he doesn't get in trouble during inspections.

RESERVE PAY

Reservists just doing their usual weekend drilling typically do four drills per weekend. Each drill is supposed to represent one day on active duty, because the military recognizes that Reservists tend to cram in a lot over that weekend. They are paid per drill based on their pay grade and cumulative years in service. Thus, an E-4 with more than two years of service gets $211 for four drills of playing warrior. Reservists also get 14 days of pay for their annual two-week stint with the Reserves, although they may get more in FSA and other allowances, depending on how far they must travel and whether or not they have a family.

A Reservist called to active duty receives the same pay and allowances as a regular active duty servicemember. However, each command determines what the Reservist deserves, including BAH and FSA—so double-check that your servicemember is getting what he should.

More important, your Reservist's military pay may be substantially less than what he was receiving in his civilian job, which he now has to leave. Prepare yourself for the prospect of active duty! Calculate the difference between your civilian and

★★★ DID YOU KNOW? ★★★

Thousands of Reservists lost all their savings when they were called to active duty in Operation Iraqi Freedom. Why? Their military pay was substantially less than their civilian pay, and they were forced to make up the difference from their own savings. Never be lulled into complacency by peacetime. Always save at least six months of the difference between military and civilian pay, in case your Reservist is called to active duty.

military pay, and save *at least* six months of that amount to use in case of an emergency.

HOW TO READ A LEAVE AND EARNINGS STATEMENT (PAY STUB)

Now that you understand the components of military pay, you can find out how much your servicemember should be earning each month by visiting *CinC*House.com's Military Pay Estimator. This powerful pay calculator has been endorsed and is used by the Navy–Marine Corps Relief Society for budget counseling purposes, so you know it gives an accurate estimate of your pay. It's also a great way to project your future income if you expect significant changes in your life, such as marriage, promotion, deployment, or relocation, or to double-check to see if DoD is paying your hardworking hubby the right amount.

Once you've calculated what your monthly pay should be, take a good look at your servicemember's pay stub, also known as a Leave and Earnings Statement (**LES**). You can also find his current LES and next month's predictions of pay on the **DFAS** (Defense Finance and Accounting Service) website at http://www.dfas.mil. Insist that your servicemember get a password for this website ASAP because you'll rely on it every time you

★★★ DID YOU KNOW? ★★★

Military pay changes as frequently as every month, depending on your servicemember's circumstances. If your servicemember does training, deploys, relocates, does hardship duty, or has any other changes in circumstances, prevent financial trouble by recalculating how much pay he should receive.

update your monthly budget and pay the bills. The total amount of your monthly income should match the Military Pay Estimator. If it does not, review each component to find the differences.

The LES will also show any **allotments.** An allotment is a certain amount of money deducted from your pay and directly paid to specified persons such as your landlord (for rent payments) or creditors. If you have bad credit, some stores will insist on being paid by allotment if you are making a large purchase.

In the old days, a deployed servicemember would set aside an allotment to his wife to ensure she had enough money to pay the bills while he was gone. Although some military financial counselors still recommend doing this, there is no reason to do so as long as the wife has access to a joint checking account that receives his pay by direct deposit. Changing a checking account or direct deposit can be done almost instantly, whereas it takes a visit to command admin and several pay periods before you can end an allotment.

On the following pages are sample Leave and Earnings Statements to show you how to interpret them.

Sample LES for Army, Navy, and Air Force

DEFENSE FINANCE AND ACCOUNTING SERVICE MILITARY LEAVE AND EARNINGS STATEMENT

ID	NAME (LAST, FIRST, MI) 1	SOC. SEC. NO. 2	GRADE 3	PAY DATE 4	YRS SVC 5	ETS 6	BRANCH 7	ADSN/DSSN 8	PERIOD COVERED 9

ENTITLEMENTS

TYPE	AMOUNT
A	
B	
C	10
D	
E	
F	
G	
H	
I	
J	
K	
L	
M	
N	
O	

DEDUCTIONS

TYPE	AMOUNT
	11

ALLOTMENTS

TYPE	AMOUNT
	12

SUMMARY

+ AMT FWD	13
+ TOT ENT	14
− TOT DED	15
− TOT ALMT	16
= NET AMT	17
− CR FWD	18
= EOM PAY	19

TOTAL 20 | 21 | 22

	DIEMS 23	RET PLAN 24

LEAVE	BF BAL 25	ERND 26	USED 27	CR BAL 28	ETS BAL 29	LV LOST 30	LV PAID 31	USE/LOSE 32

FED TAXES	WAGE PERIOD 33	WAGE YTD 34	M/S 35	EX 36	ADD'L TAX 37	TAX YTD 38

FICA TAXES	WAGE PERIOD 39	SOC WAGE YTD 40	SOC TAX YTD 41	MED WAGE YTD 42	MED TAX YTD 43

STATE TAXES	ST 44	WAGE PERIOD 45	WAGE YTD 46	M/S 47	EX 48	TAX YTD 49

PAY DATA	BAQ TYPE 50	BAQ DEPN 51	VHA ZIP 52	RENT AMT 53	SHARE 54	STAT 55	JFTR 56	DEPNS 57	2D JFTR 58	BAS TYPE 59	CHARITY YTD 60	TPC 61	PACIDN 62

Thrift Savings Plan (TSP)	BASE PAY RATE 63	BASE PAY CURRENT 64	SPEC PAY RATE 65	SPEC PAY CURRENT 66	INC PAY RATE 67	INC PAY CURRENT 68	BONUS PAY RATE 69	BONUS PAY CURRENT 70
	CURRENTLY NOT USED 71	TSP YTD DEDUCTIONS 72	DEFERRED 73	EXEMPT 74	CURRENTLY NOT USED 75			

REMARKS 76

YTD ENTITLE 77

YTD DEDUCT 78

DFAS Form 702, Jan 02

www.dfas.mil

Source: DFAS

74

Fields 1–9 contain the identification portion of the LES.

1. NAME. The member's name in last, first, middle initial format.
2. SOC. SEC. NO. The member's Social Security number.
3. GRADE. The member's current pay grade.
4. PAY DATE. The date the member entered active duty for pay purposes in YYMMDD format. This is synonymous with the Pay Entry Base Date (PEBD).
5. YRS SVC. In two digits, the actual years of creditable service.
6. ETS. The Expiration Term of Service in YYMMDD format. This is synonymous with the Expiration of Active Obligated Service (EAOS).
7. BRANCH. The branch of service, i.e., Navy, Army, Air Force.
8. ADSN/DSSN. The Disbursing Station Symbol Number used to identify each disbursing/finance office.
9. PERIOD COVERED. This is the period covered by the individual LES. Normally, it will be for one calendar month. If this is a separation LES, the separation date will appear in this field.

Fields 10–24 contain the entitlements, deductions, allotments, and their respective totals; a mathematical summary portion; date initially entered military service; and retirement plan.

10. ENTITLEMENTS. In columnar style, the names of the entitlements and allowances being paid. Space is allocated for 15 entitlements and/or allowances. If more than 15 are present, the overflow will be printed in the REMARKS block. Any retroactive entitlements and/or allowances will be added to like entitlements and/or allowances.
11. DEDUCTIONS. The descriptions of the deductions are listed in columnar style. This includes items such as taxes, SGLI, mid-month pay, and dependent dental plan. Space is allocated for 15 deductions. If more than 15 are present, the overflow will be printed in the REMARKS block. Any retroactive deductions will be added to like deductions.
12. ALLOTMENTS. In columnar style, the type of the actual allotments being deducted. This includes discretionary and nondiscre-

tionary allotments for savings and/or checking accounts, insurance, bonds, etc. Space is allocated for 15 allotments. If a member has more than one of the same type of allotment, the only differentiation may be that of the dollar amount.

13. + AMT FWD. The amount of all unpaid pay and allowances due from the prior LES.

14. + TOT ENT. The figure from Field 20, which is the total of all entitlements and/or allowances listed.

15. – TOT DED. The figure from Field 21, which is the total of all deductions.

16. – TOT ALMT. The figure from Field 22, which is the total of all allotments.

17. = NET AMT. The dollar value of all unpaid pay and allowances, plus total entitlements and/or allowances, minus deductions and allotments due on the current LES.

18. – CR FWD. The dollar value of all unpaid pay and allowances due to reflect on the next LES as the + AMT FWD.

19. = EOM PAY. The actual amount of the payment to be paid to the member on end-of-month payday.

20–22. TOTAL. The total amounts for the entitlements and/or allowances, deductions, and allotments, respectively.

23. DIEMS. Date initially entered military service: This date is used *solely* to indicate which retirement plan a member is under. For those members with a DIEMS date prior to September 8, 1980, they are under the Final Pay retirement plan. For those members with a DIEMS date of September 8, 1980, through July 31, 1986, they are under the High-3 retirement plan. For those members with a DIEMS date of August 1, 1986, or later, they were initially under the REDUX retirement plan. This was changed by law in October 2000, when they were placed under the High-3 plan, with the option to return to the REDUX plan. In consideration of making this election, they become entitled to a $30,000 Career Status Bonus. The data in this block comes from PERSCOM. DFAS is not responsible for the accuracy of this data. If a member feels that the DIEMS date shown in this block is erroneous, he must see his local servicing personnel office for corrective action.

24. RET PLAN. Type of retirement plan, i.e., Final Pay, High-3, REDUX, or Choice. (Choice reflects members who have less than 15 years service and have not elected to go with REDUX or stay with their current retirement plan.)

Fields 25–32 contain leave information.

25. BF BAL. The brought-forward leave balance. Balance may be from the beginning of the fiscal year, or when active duty began, or the day after the member was paid Lump Sum Leave (LSL).
26. ERND. The cumulative amount of leave earned in the current fiscal year or current term of enlistment if the member reenlisted/extended since the beginning of the fiscal year. Normally increases by 2.5 days each month.
27. USED. The cumulative amount of leave used in the current fiscal year or current term of enlistment if member reenlisted/extended since the beginning of the fiscal year.
28. CR BAL. The current leave balance as of the end of the period covered by the LES.
29. ETS BAL. The projected leave balance to the member's Expiration Term of Service (ETS).
30. LV LOST. The number of days of leave that have been lost.
31. LV PAID. The number of days of leave paid to date.
32. USE/LOSE. The projected number of days of leave that will be lost if not taken in the current fiscal year on a monthly basis. The number of days of leave in this block will decrease with any leave usage.

Fields 33–38 contain federal tax withholding information.

33. WAGE PERIOD. The amount of money earned this LES period that is subject to Federal Income Tax Withholding (FITW).
34. WAGE YTD. The money earned year-to-date that is subject to FITW.
35. M/S. The marital status used to compute the FITW.
36. EX. The number of exemptions used to compute the FITW.

37. ADD'L TAX. The member-specified additional dollar amount to be withheld in addition to the amount computed by the marital status and exemptions.

38. TAX YTD. The cumulative total of FITW withheld throughout the calendar year.

Fields 39–43 contain Federal Insurance Contributions Act (FICA) information.

39. WAGE PERIOD. The amount of money earned this LES period that is subject to FICA.

40. SOC WAGE YTD. The wages earned year-to-date that are subject to FICA.

41. SOC TAX YTD. Cumulative total of FICA withheld throughout the calendar year.

42. MED WAGE YTD. The wages earned year-to-date that are subject to Medicare.

43. MED TAX YTD. Cumulative total of Medicare taxes paid year-to-date.

Fields 44–49 contain state tax information.

44. ST. The two-digit postal abbreviation for the state the member elected.

45. WAGE PERIOD. The amount of money earned this LES period that is subject to State Income Tax Withholding (SITW).

46. WAGE YTD. The money earned year-to-date that is subject to SITW.

47. M/S. The marital status used to compute the SITW.

48. EX. The number of exemptions used to compute the SITW.

49. TAX YTD. The cumulative total of SITW withheld throughout the calendar year.

Fields 50–62 contain additional pay data.

50. BAQ TYPE. The type of Basic Allowance for Quarters being paid.

51. BAQ DEPN. A code that indicates the type of dependent.

A—Spouse

C—Child

D—Parent

G—Grandparent

I—Member married to member/own right

K—Ward of the court

L—Parents-in-law

R—Own right

S—Student (ages 21–22)

T—Handicapped child over age 21

W—Member married to member, child under age 21

52. VHA ZIP. The zip code used in the computation of Variable Housing Allowance (VHA), if entitlement exists.

53. RENT AMT. The amount of rent paid for housing, if applicable.

54. SHARE. The number of people with whom the member shares housing costs.

55. STAT. The VHA status; i.e., accompanied or unaccompanied.

56. JFTR. The Joint Federal Travel Regulation (JFTR) code, based on the location of the member for Cost of Living Allowance (COLA) purposes.

57. DEPNS. The number of dependents the member has for VHA purposes.

58. 2D JFTR. The JFTR code, based on the location of the member's dependents for COLA purposes.

59. BAS TYPE. An alpha code that indicates the type of Basic Allowance for Subsistence (BAS) the member is receiving, if applicable. This field will be blank for officers.

B—Separate Rations

C—TDY/PCS/Proceed Time

H—Rations-in-kind not available

K—Rations under emergency conditions

60. CHARITY YTD. The cumulative amount of charitable contributions for the calendar year.

61. TPC. This field is not used by the active component of any branch of service.

62. PACIDN. The activity Unit Identification Code (UIC). This field is currently used by Army only.

Fields 63–75 contain Thrift Savings Plan (TSP) information/data.

63. BASE PAY RATE. The percentage of base pay elected for TSP contributions.

64. BASE PAY CURRENT. Reserved for future use.

65. SPECIAL PAY RATE. The percentage of Special Pay elected for TSP contributions.

66. SPECIAL PAY CURRENT. Reserved for future use.

67. INCENTIVE PAY RATE. Percentage of Incentive Pay elected for TSP contributions.

68. INCENTIVE PAY CURRENT. Reserved for future use.

69. BONUS PAY RATE. The percentage of Bonus Pay elected toward TSP contributions.

70. BONUS PAY CURRENT. Reserved for future use.

71. Reserved for future use.

72. TSP YTD DEDUCTION. Dollar amount of TSP contributions deducted for the year to date.

73. DEFERRED. Total dollar amount of TSP contributions that are deferred for tax purposes.

74. EXEMPT. Dollar amount of TSP contributions that are reported as tax exempt to the Internal Revenue Service.

75. Reserved for future use.

76. REMARKS. This area is used to provide you with general notices from varying levels of command, as well as the literal explanation of starts, stops, and changes to pay items in the entries within the ENTITLEMENTS, DEDUCTIONS, and ALLOTMENTS fields.

77. YTD ENTITLE. The cumulative total of all entitlements for the calendar year.

78. YTD DEDUCT. The cumulative total of all deductions for the calendar year.

Sample LES for the Marine Corps

MARINE CORPS TOTAL FORCE LEAVE AND EARNINGS STATEMENT

| A ID DIST RUC INFO | 1 NAME (LAST, FIRST, MI) | 2 SSN | 3 RANK | 4 SERV | 5 PLT CODE | 6 DATE PREP | 7 PRD COVERED | 8 PEBD | 9 YRS | 0 EAS | 11 ECC | 12 MCC |

| B FORCAST AMOUNTS | 13 DATE | 14 DATE | AMOUNT | | | 16 AMOUNT | 17 BALANCE | 18 POE | D DIRECT DEPOSIT/EFT/ADDRESS |

E LEAVE INFORMATION

| 19 LV BF EARNED USED INFORMATION | 20 | 21 | 22 EXCESS | 23 BAL | 24 MAX ACCRUAL | 25 | 26 LOST | SO LDHS OF | 27 CBT LV BAL | 28 OFFICER BASE DATE | 29 AVIATOR BASE DATE | 30 | 31 ACCUM OP FLY TIME YRS MO | 32 OP FLY TIME BASE DATE |

C SPLIT PAY (column under AMOUNT)

F AVIATION PAY INFORMATION

G GOVERNMENT — **TAX INFORMATION**

| 33 STATE TAX | 34 FEDERAL TAX | 35 FICA (SOCIAL SECURITY TAX) |

STATE CODE
EXEMPTIONS   EXEMPTIONS   SEC WAGES THIS PRD
WAGES YTD   WAGES YTD   SEC WAGES YTD
STATE TAX YTD   FED TAX YTD   SEC TAX YTD   MEDICARE WAGES THIS PRD
                                        MEDICARE WAGES YTD
                                        MEDICARE TAX YTD

H RIGHTS OF MARINES INDEBTED TO THE

YOU HAVE THE RIGHT TO:
—Inspect and copy records pertaining to debt
—Question validity of a debt and submit refuting evidence
—Negotiate a repayment schedule
—Request a waiver of debt

More information about your rights can be obtained from your Commanding Officer via your Chain of Command.

I INFO — **ADDITIONAL BAH INFORMATION**

| 36 | 37 BAH ZIP | 38 | 39 | 40 | 41 | 42 |

| J CARRIER SEA PAY | 43 DATE TOTAL CARRIER SEA SVC |

| K EDUCATION DEDUCTION | 44 TYPE YRS MO DA | 45 MONTHLY AMT | 46 TOTAL | 47 PAY STATUS | L ADMIN |

| 48 PAY | 49 CBA DATE GROUP | M RESERVE DRILL INFORMATION |

| | | 55 ADD | 56 ADD | 57 BF | 58 ACDU | 59 DRILL | 60 OTHER | 61 MBR | 62 END BAL | 63 TOTAL | 64 TOTAL | 65 |

| 52 REG | 53 REG | 54 ADD | ADD ANNYTD | ADD FYTD | | | | | | N RESERVE RETIREMENT INFORMATION |

REG 51	REG 52	ADD 54	ADD 55	ADD 56	BF 57	ACDU 58	DRILL 59	OTHER 60	MBR 61	END BAL 62	TOTAL 63	TOTAL 64	65
DSSN	ANNYTD	FYTD	ANNYTD	ANNYTD	ANNYTD	THIS PRD	THIS PRD	THIS PRD	THIS PRD	ANNYTD	SAT YRS	RET PTS	RESERVE ECC

| 50 |

O REMARKS

DFAS-KC 7220/39 (REV 2-9)   WWW.DFAS.MIL   EFT INFO-DFAS-KC 1-800-449-3327

Source: DFAS

81

The Marine Corps LES has a slightly different format than the other services, but the same acronyms and categories apply.

TAXABLE VS. NONTAXABLE INCOME

It may seem like nitpicking, but it's important to know how much of your income is taxable vs. nontaxable because it affects your tax withholding and helps you compare a military salary against a civilian salary. To determine an equivalent civilian salary, multiply your nontaxable income by approximately 30 percent—or the amount the government would tax you—and add that to your total salary. For example, if your servicemember earns $15,000 per year in taxable income and $15,000 per year in nontaxable income, he is actually earning the civilian equivalent of $34,500—not $30,000. You can also get tax benefits from certain states. If you live in Virginia, for example, your servicemember will not owe any state taxes because the first $15,000 in pay is not taxed.

PROBLEMS WITH MILITARY PAY

Like all human beings, the military bureaucracy sometimes makes mistakes in pay. It is in your best interest to watch out for overpayments as well as underpayments. Whatever you do, do not spend an overpayment, because someday the government will find out, and it will dock your pay the full amount until the money is paid back. Many a family has walked into financial counseling because they weren't aware of an overpayment—or multiple overpayments—and were docked pay for months at a time because they couldn't pay it back.

Pay miscalculations happen in all components of military pay, but especially in those areas that change during relocation and deployment. If you think you have a pay problem, start by determining how much you should be paid on the *CinC*House.com Military Pay Estimator. Cross-check that amount on your servicemember's LES. If you find a discrepancy, have your hubby verify and correct it immediately with his command admin, who will work with your personnel office or the Disbursement Office, both of which work with DFAS's central office. Finally, if you find yourself in a pickle because of an accounting error, visit a financial services organization such as the Navy–Marine Corps Relief Society. It can provide you with an interest-free loan to help you survive paying back money or cover you in the case of underpayment.

DIRECT DEPOSIT

In this day and age, everyone should be receiving his or her pay via direct deposit into a checking account, but this is particularly important for military families. Some special pays and bonuses, particularly those related to relocation, temporary duty, and deployment, are not paid in advance with your biweekly paycheck. Instead, they are often paid at the last minute. With direct deposit, you are ensuring the money goes directly into your checking account when you need it instead of worrying about when—or whether—a check will arrive in the mail before you begin traveling.

TAX AND REGULATORY BENEFITS

As you may have noticed with the example of state income taxes, many states treat military servicemembers quite favorably when it comes to other taxes and regulations. Automobiles and state residency are the biggest examples. Armed with this knowledge, you can take advantage of the benefits.

Your servicemember's state residency should be a matter of

financial savvy, not emotional attachment to his hometown. Military servicemembers are exempt from having to reestablish their legal residency every time they move, so they can choose their legal state of residence, even if they haven't lived there in 20 years or if they initially lived there for only a few months. The key to establishing legal residency is getting a driver's license and registering to vote in that particular state. Many servicemembers deliberately establish their residence in states such as Florida, Texas, and Pennsylvania in order to avoid paying high income taxes elsewhere, particularly in states such as California.

Military spouses are not so lucky. We are forced to change our state residency every time we relocate and pay taxes in that state. This causes more problems than just having to calculate taxes for two states in a year in which you have relocated. If a car is registered or coregistered in your name, you are required to reregister it in your new state and pay taxes on it. For this reason, many military couples opt to keep their cars in the servicemember's name only. Again, the servicemember will carefully select a state of residence that has low automobile taxes.

Going back to the issue of financial benefits for hazardous duty, servicemembers receive significant tax relief if the Internal Revenue Service (IRS) deems them as performing "qualified haz-

★★★ DID YOU KNOW? ★★★

Most couples opt to register property such as cars in the name of a servicemember only to prevent having to reregister the vehicles and pay higher taxes with every move. If you think you may be headed for divorce, however, change the registration to list yourself as co-owner. While most divorce courts will recognize the spouse as co-owner, it's better to be safe than sorry.

ardous duty" in a designated Combat Zone. This exemption is called the "Combat Tax Exclusion" and is determined by Congress or the President. Typically, this status is designated for wartime or dangerous peacekeeping operations, and it means that all enlisted and warrant officer pay earned while in that duty station is not subject to federal and state income tax. Officers' pay not subject to tax is capped at the highest amount of enlisted pay plus Imminent Danger Pay, and the rest is taxable. So if your hubby spent six months at Operation Joint Guard in Bosnia-Herzegovina or in other designated dangerous locations such as Afghanistan or the Persian Gulf, none or little of his pay for that time can be taxed by the IRS. Check the IRS website at http://www.irs.gov or with command admin to make sure he is qualified.

LOWER YOUR INTEREST RATES BY GOING TO WAR

The Soldiers' and Sailors' Civil Relief Act (SSCRA) can also bring you a reduction in your mortgage interest rates and other loans—a critical savings for Reservists in particular, since they are most likely to see their income plummet when they leave their civilian jobs and go on active duty for an extended period. When the SSCRA is invoked during wartime or near-wartime situations, the Department of Housing and Urban Development (HUD) sends a letter to all FHA-approved mortgage lenders advising them of their obligations under this act, namely that they must reduce their mortgage interest rates to no more than 6 percent for loans to military on active duty (including Guard and Reserve). The SSCRA also:

★ Prohibits lenders from foreclosing on servicemembers during and immediately following their tour of active duty.
★ Reduces rates on preexisting credit card debt to 6 percent.
★ Prevents eviction if your rent is less than $1,200 per month.

★ Can delay all civil court proceedings, including bankruptcy and divorce.

The military recommends that you send notice in writing to all lenders if you plan to invoke the 6 percent cap on interest rates, and keep a copy for yourself. For more information, call HUD at 1-888-297-8685 or go to the HUD website at www.hud.gov.

RETIREMENT BENEFITS

Servicemembers on active duty or in the Reserves or Guard may retire with pensionlike benefits after a certain period of time, typically after 20 years of service. Disabled servicemembers may also be medically retired prior to 20 years. Simply leaving active duty after five years of service does not make you a "retiree." Retirees receive monthly income from the government for life and may continue to receive important benefits, such as medical care and access to services on base.

There are effectively two retirement systems available for nondisability retirees. First is the **High-3** Year Average system, which entitles a servicemember to receive a percentage of his Basic Pay at his last pay grade as calculated by 2.5 percent times the number of years in services. For example, if your servicemember serves 30 years, he would receive 2.5% × 30, or 75 percent, of his average Basic Pay received during the 36 months when it was highest. Cost-of-living adjustments (COLA) are increased annually to account for the increase in inflation.

The **REDUX** retirement system is more controversial because it offers a $30,000 Career Status Bonus to servicemembers in their 15th year of employment if they commit to 20 years of service. Those who don't complete that commitment must pay back a prorated share of the bonus. The bonus is considered to be taxable income unless placed in a tax-free investment, such as an Individual Retirement Account (IRA). The retirement multiplier is reduced to 2 percent for those serving 20 years, although it goes back up to 2.5 percent for those serving as long as 30 years. However, at age 62, the retirement multiplier is recalculated to come on par with the High-3 multiplier. And the COLA is less than what is offered in High-3, effectively the inflation rate (Consumer Price Index or CPI) minus 1 percent.

In the end, those who accept REDUX over the High-3 retirement system must decide early—at the 15-year mark in their career—that they plan to stay for the full 30 years in order to maximize their benefits. Further, they take on the added risk that the COLA may not keep up with the pace of inflation, so their personal retirement savings would have to cover the gap through the duration of their retirement. The key is to ask yourself whether you would invest the $30,000 bonus or spend it. Investing it ensures your long-term retirement income and possibly an inheritance for your child; spending the money could spell disaster and poverty for REDUX retirees. So be honest with yourself and talk to a financial planner before making this important choice.

The Thrift Savings Plan (**TSP**) is an additional and voluntary retirement savings plan originally created for federal civilian employees and extended to military servicemembers in 2000. It is ultimately intended to replace the old retirement system by acting like a 401(k) plan. Every year, your servicemember puts away a certain amount of money, up to 7 percent of Basic Pay and 100 percent of Special and Bonus Pay, in a specified mutual fund monitored by the TSP administrators. There are five mutual funds to choose from, ranging from conservative to aggressive in their approach and rate of return. The money invested is not taxed as income that year, which reduces your tax burden, and over time your retirement savings grow in the private stock and bond markets. The income you receive in retirement depends upon how much you have invested and your rate of return, and you will receive those benefits no matter when you retire or leave the military.

TSP is not a perfect retirement plan in that it doesn't allow spouses to participate and the government does not match most servicemembers' contributions dollar for dollar, the way many civilian employers do. But it's a terrific way to ensure you and your hubby have enough money to retire someday, even if Congress doesn't fully fund the retirement benefits you were promised. For more information, visit http://www.tsp.gov.

HOW POLITICS AFFECTS YOUR RETIREMENT

Did you notice that, in the creation and emphasis of the REDUX system over the High-3 system, the Department of Defense is trying to "pre-load" your retirement savings so that the stock market—and not taxpayer money—is funding your retirement? That's because, within the next 30 years, the federal government will no longer be able to afford to pay for all of the retirement promises it has made to employees and Social Security recipients. Instead, they are hoping everyone will create their own retirement savings to fund each individual retirement, rather than rely on a DoD pension or Social Security benefit.

It sounds insane to offer such massive retirement benefits that you cannot afford to pay out—but that's Congress for you. And Congress is now scrambling to fix the problem. Unfortunately, Congress is also responsible for the yearly cost-of-living adjustments (COLAs) that are supposed to increase your retirement income to keep up with inflation. The reality, however, is that COLAs decrease when the military is not politically popular and increase when it is. As the population of veterans decreases with the passing of the World War II generation, be aware that your retirement benefits may wane with the political will of Congress. In the end, you need to save for your own retirement.

SURVIVOR'S BENEFITS AND LIFE INSURANCE

While the military does not provide a retirement savings option for military spouses, it does provide some survivor's benefits to spouses of military personnel who die on active duty or when death is due to a service-related disability.

The Dependency and Indemnity Compensation (DIC) program at the Veterans Administration provides benefits to surviving family members under special circumstances. However, the average survivor benefit under this program is only $6,000 per year!

What this means is that **you need to have life insurance and save for your own retirement—no one else will do it for you.**

Certainly, it is difficult for spouses to save for retirement. Because we move from job to job, we're not likely to contribute to employer-sponsored retirement investments such as a 401(k) plan for any length of time. *CinC*House *strongly* encourages you to set up your own IRA and invest in it *at least* the same amount of money your husband invests in his retirement savings plan or TSP.

Once you enter military life, you will be bombarded with offers for inexpensive life insurance for you and your service-member. It's enough to make you wonder why.

While choosing life insurance is a complicated and personal

2000 "IMPROVED" DEATH PENSION

Recipient	Maximum Annual Rate
Veteran with one dependent	$11,773
Veteran permanently housebound with one dependent	$13,771
Surviving spouse	$6,026
with one child	$7,891
Surviving spouse permanently housebound	$7,367
with one child	$9,228
Surviving spouse needing regular assistance	$9,635
with one child	$11,497
Allowance for each additional child	$1,532
Pension for each surviving child	$1,532

Source: "Federal Benefits for Veterans and Dependents," 2000 Edition, Veterans Administration

decision, partly because it can be treated as an investment opportunity, you should know that the military provides very inexpensive life insurance for your entire family through the duration of service. The program, entitled Servicemembers' Group Life Insurance (**SGLI**), provides $250,000 in coverage to active duty servicemembers for just $16.25 per month. For spouses, SGLI provides $100,000 coverage for $9 per month for ages 34 and below, and $13 per month for ages 35–44, and so on, past this age bracket. Dependent children automatically receive $10,000 coverage free of charge. While you may want to consider purchasing life insurance that extends beyond the duration of your servicemember's service, you'd be hard-pressed to beat these rates for your immediate needs.

EDUCATIONAL BENEFITS

When most people think of educational opportunities related to the military, they think of the Montgomery G.I. Bill. This is the recruiting incentive that offers most active duty servicemembers and Reservists up to $28,800 in tuition in return for a three-year commitment on active duty. During that commitment, you pay $100 a month for a year, but you will get up to $985 a month for three years, which can be put to use not only for college degree programs but also for certificate programs, flight training, apprenticeship/on-the-job training, and correspondence courses.

The Student Loan Repayment Program is the reverse of the Montgomery G.I. Bill, effectively paying off your student loan in return for a service commitment. And as long as it was a federally insured student loan, the loan could even have come from your parents!

In addition to these great opportunities, however, the military boasts a network of more than 300 schools and 10,000 courses for servicemembers, a number of which count as college credit and are also available to spouses. That does not include the hundreds of colleges and universities that maintain representatives and/or courses on each base, nor the opportunities for distance learning, nor the hundreds of scholarships available to servicemembers and their spouses and children.

In the end, there is almost no excuse for any military wife or woman not to complete or continue her education. To get a list of local colleges and universities, especially those with representatives on your local military base, visit *CinC*House.com's sections on local military bases or call the career counselor at your local Family Support Center. Also, visit *CinC*House.com periodically for an update of the latest scholarship opportunities available for you or your children.

The Least You Need to Know

★ Understand the components of military pay and find out how your servicemember's pay will vary depending on your circumstances. Don't be caught off guard by a $200 pay short.

★ Check your Leave and Earnings Statement each month and compare it to the *CinC*House Military Pay Estimator to see if you have any overpayments or pay shorts. Report any pay problems immediately to your command admin, and be sure not to spend any overpayments.

★ Military servicemembers receive substantial tax and regulatory benefits and creditor protections, but you have to learn about them in order to maximize your money.

★ If your servicemember plans to make a career of the military, he should choose his retirement plan carefully to make sure it fits your spending habits and retirement needs.

★ The Social Security and military pension systems may be going bankrupt, so it's important that you and your servicemember save money for retirement through the Thrift Savings Program and Individual Retirement Accounts.

★ Survivor benefits for widows are a pittance, so make sure you purchase life insurance and save money of your own.

Resources

★ http://www.cinchouse.com—Find the Military Pay Estimator to calculate how much income your servicemember should be receiving each month depending on his circumstances.

★ http://www.dfas.mil—Bookmark this link to the Defense Finance and Accounting Service! You'll use this site to check your servicemember's monthly Leave and Earnings Statements, predict next month's pay, and fix any pay problems.

★ *The Savvy Sailor* (http://www.savvy.onweb.com)—This terrific book explains the details of military financial planning while telling a romantic story of a couple who fall in love and get married. Even though it's written for sailors, all servicemembers can benefit.

★ http://www.hud.gov—The Department of Housing and Urban Development has more information on how you can receive financial protection and lower your interest rates under the Soldiers' and Sailors' Civil Relief Act.

★ http://www.irs.gov—The Internal Revenue Service website provides specific information for military families on how to reduce your tax burden. Make it a point to visit this site before you do your taxes every year.

★ http://www.tsp.gov—More information on the Thrift Savings Program, which your servicemember should be using to save money for retirement.

8

Health Care Benefits

For servicemembers on active duty, the military promises them and their families virtually free health care and generally delivers. Nowhere else in the world can you deliver a baby with complete pre- and postnatal care at absolutely no cost. This care is delivered through Tricare, the military's own HMO. While some might think Tricare has a bottomless pit of funding from Congress, the program administration is actually assisted by regional private HMOs that contract with the government. As with all HMOs, getting the best medical care means understanding the system.

MYTHS ABOUT MILITARY VS. CIVILIAN CARE

The first thing you'll discover about military health care is that there are military doctors and hospitals. While Tricare will allow you to see a civilian provider if you live more than 50 miles from a military base, it will typically assign you a military primary care physician if you have signed up for Tricare Prime.

Oh, great! you think. The same bozos who keep me waiting in line to sign papers are now providing my health care!

Actually, military doctors and nurses are exactly the same as their civilian counterparts, except they know more about military-specific issues, deploy with the troops, and relocate as frequently as you do. Doctors train in the same medical schools as civilian providers, but instead of owing hundreds of thousands in student loans—paid for by patients like you—they are debt-free in exchange for serving time in the military. Lack of school debt means doctors can make medical decisions entirely free, consciously or unconsciously, of financial incentives.

In addition to going through regular medical training, military doctors and health care providers receive extra schooling in subjects like tropical diseases and biological/chemical threats. Extra training has benefits for you, from understanding how to treat the rash your child got while in Guam to providing the first response to biological warfare with antidotes they keep on hand in their hospitals.

★★★ **WAR STORIES** ★★★

Where to Go on September 11

September 11 was a terrifying day for all Americans, and many spent the following weeks trying to find gas masks and determine which drugs they needed to stock their medicine cabinet. Talk radio hosts pondered for hours where citizens could go to protect themselves.

Most military wives had no such doubts. Not only was base security searching anything that moved, our hospitals and clinics were already stocked with antidotes to biological threats like anthrax and teaming with the best-trained medical experts in the world. Besides, I defy any terrorist to go directly after a U.S. military base, especially one housing the Marines. The relish with which the Marines would respond brings a smile to my face just thinking about it.

Finally, military doctors understand what you're going through in terms of relocation, deployment, and other issues because they go through it, too. My own case is a good example of the special treatment we get in unusual circumstances. My husband and I had trouble conceiving our first child. After trying for the requisite one year, we had only three months left before we were scheduled to relocate to a training program across the country. Recognizing the trouble we would have had starting up with a new gynecologist at this stage, my gynecologist (an expert in infertility) expedited the tests and procedures needed to get me knocked up before we relocated. Two weeks before the movers came, I found out I was pregnant, and we now have a beautiful baby boy!

While there is a priority system whereby servicemembers are treated first, followed by families and then veterans, enlisted family members benefit the most because the system is designed to serve young families. Your primary care physician will probably be a family practitioner, sometimes called a "super GP" because they handle everything from delivering babies to well-baby checkups, but have significantly more training than the old-fashioned general practitioners. With family practitioners, you can make one appointment for the whole family and see the same doctor every time (unless you or the doctor relocates).

Alternative medicine and nontraditional providers, including chiropractors, acupuncturists, and nurse midwives, are respected and widespread at military hospitals. Some nurse practitioners are even trained by the military in acupuncture and other holistic medicine.

Finally, the military's use of training hospitals to provide care for military families means that military doctors are on the cutting edge of medicine. As a patient, you'll receive care based on the latest scientific knowledge and best equipment.

TRICARE: THE HMO FOR THE MILITARY

The reason you need to understand that there are virtually no differences—and some benefits—to having a military health care provider is that such care costs substantially less than insisting upon a civilian provider.

Tricare has two main types of health plans for active duty family members: Tricare Prime and Tricare Standard. Active duty servicemembers themselves are covered under Prime, as are most military families. Reservists are covered by Tricare only if they are activated, and then they and their families receive the same coverage as active duty—but be sure to jump on the paperwork to start coverage right away.

Tricare Prime works much like a typical HMO. There are no enrollment fees, deductibles, or cost sharing (except overseas), but you are required to go through the military health system first and, if care is not available, only then can you see a civilian provider. What that means is that you must attempt to receive care through a Primary Care Manager (**PCM**) at a Military Treatment Facility (**MTF**) such as a Uniformed Services Hospital or clinic. If they cannot provide you care, you must request that they issue a Nonavailability Statement (NAS) in order for you to receive treatment at a civilian facility. *Without the NAS, you will be fully responsible for all costs associated with civilian care.* You can find a civilian provider authorized by Tricare in your area by looking on the Tricare website at http://tma.osd. mil, reviewing its provider booklet, calling your local Tricare representative, or, if overseas, asking the local U.S. embassy or consulate. Under Prime, you can receive emergency care in any military or civilian facility, but you should check and notify your MTF and/or Tricare representative. Similarly, specialty care—provided by both military and civilians—is available, but it must be managed and coordinated through your PCM. Now you understand the importance of building a good relationship with your PCM! Tricare Prime coverage is portable as you move from region to region (see regions and contact information on pages 104–6).

In contrast to Tricare Prime, Tricare Standard is less popular among military families because of the deductibles and cost sharing as well as more restricted access to care at a military facility. Also, unlike Prime, you or your health care provider must file your claims in order to subsequently be reimbursed, which means you may be carrying health care expenses on your credit card for a while. Tricare Standard is generally preferred by wives who want to continue using a specific civilian provider and who have other health insurance provided by their employer. Whenever Tricare beneficiaries carry a second form of insurance, Tricare becomes the secondary payer (once the annual deductible is paid) and typically covers whatever out-of-pocket expenses are not covered by the employer's insurance. Without the second form of insurance, however, Tricare pays only 80 percent of the authorized cost, and you pay the remaining 20 percent plus any fees that are higher than what Tricare authorizes (up to the legal limit of 15 percent above Tricare rates). Tricare Standard does have a cap on what you pay out-of-pocket for catastrophic care, so long as the services are authorized, but you must keep close track of your expenses.

Special plans for special situations are also available under Tricare, such as Tricare Prime Remote. This is the equivalent of Tricare Prime for beneficiaries who live 50 miles or one hour away from the closest MTF.

Pharmacy benefits are also included in both Tricare plans. Your out-of-pocket costs for prescription drugs are zero if you obtain your prescription at an MTF pharmacy, and you can receive the full amount on the prescription. The second option is the Tricare Mail Order Pharmacy, but you can get only a 90-day supply of your prescription at a time. Contact your health care provider, or call 1-866-363-8667 in the U.S. or 1-866-275-4732 overseas to find out more. A third option is to use a Tricare network pharmacy, which includes most major drugstore chains. You will pay $9 for a 30-day supply of a brand-name medica-

TRICARE COST COMPARISON CHART

	Tricare Prime	Tricare Standard
Annual Deductible	None	$150 per individual or $300 per family for E-5 and above; $50/$100 for E-4 and below
Annual Enrollment Fee	None	None
Civilian Outpatient Visit	No cost with NAS	20% of allowable charge plus any costs above allowable charge (up to 15%)
Civilian Inpatient Admission	No cost	$25 flat fee or $11.90 per day, whichever is greater
Civilian Inpatient Mental Health	No cost	$20 per day

Source: The Tricare Handbook

tion, or $3 for a 30-day supply of the generic version. Finally, you can use a non-network pharmacy, but you will be reimbursed for only 80 percent of the cost *after* your annual deductible is paid. Again, it pays to use a military health facility.

HOW TRICARE'S COVERAGE RATES

Having spent ten years in and out of different HMOs paid for by my civilian employers, I can attest that Tricare appears to have the same caliber of health care coverage—and often better. Government health benefits usually are. Those who complain about Tricare typically have unusual circumstances or don't understand and aren't willing to deal with the HMO system. HMOs are here to stay, folks, and Tricare is one of the better ones.

The key to obtaining coverage of your specific health care needs is the term "medically necessary." Tricare has a list of what ailments are or are not covered, but if a doctor says you need coverage, Tricare will generally give it. Military doctors and civilians who do a lot of work with Tricare understand this, and they will work with you to make sure your expenses are covered. Yet another reason to establish a good relationship with your PCM!

To my knowledge, Tricare Prime is the only HMO plan in the world where it costs absolutely nothing to have a baby, from your prenatal vitamins to your postpartum checkup. Well-baby, well-child, and well-woman visits are also covered, as are visits for mental health care, obesity, infertility, birth control, and genetic testing. There are some exceptions to coverage, such as artificial insemination and abortion (unless the mother's health is at risk), but much of it is left to the discretion of your doctor.

Maternity care is particularly generous and hassle-free under Tricare. To obtain a civilian provider and pay no addi-

★★★ **DID YOU KNOW?** ★★★

Once you give birth, your baby is automatically covered by Tricare for the first 120 days of life. At that point, your servicemember must enroll the child in DEERS, which amends the Page 2 of his service record to explain his expanding family, and complete a Tricare Prime enrollment form. Don't forget to do this, or you'll be kicking yourself when your child is suddenly not eligible to see his or her doctor and you have to go through a bureaucratic hassle to rectify this.

tional costs, you need only a Nonavailability Statement from your local MTF, and then you need to find a health care provider and facility that are part of the Tricare network. If you wish to use alternative methods, such as a birthing facility instead of a hospital, you have the option to do so, but with costs being shared. The only outstanding item not covered is "lay" midwives (as opposed to the medically trained and licensed superhero nurse midwives), but no insurance covers such minimally trained, nonlicensed caregivers.

On a final note, be sure to verify your Tricare coverage and DEERS report every year or every time you move. These guys process up to 25 million claims each year and are known for occasionally "dropping" beneficiaries out of the system. This comes as a shock when the purported beneficiary is either denied care or receives a whopping bill for health services. A once-per-year verification is worth the trouble of a phone call compared to a bureaucratic nightmare of a dropped beneficiary.

TRICKS FOR GETTING THE BEST HEALTH CARE

As with all HMOs, there are tricks to avoiding bureaucrats and getting the best health care available. Fortunately, as discussed earlier, the system is designed to try to connect you with one family provider instead of allowing you to slip through the cracks by using multiple doctors. By trying to stick with one doctor, you can build a relationship of trust so you can deal directly with him or her when issues come up instead of always having to make an appointment. Should you have an emergency, be sure to keep your family doctor informed. And should your doctor relocate, ask him or her to refer you to another doctor. You are more likely to get someone who operates along the same lines of your old doctor.

Getting personal referrals from friends and neighbors for your family health care provider can help you identify one provider, among hundreds at any military hospital, who will understand your needs. Only once you've identified a provider, *then* call Tricare to designate him or her as your Primary Care Manager and make an appointment.

What should you do if you don't like your doctor? Switch! Ask your friends and neighbors whom they use and call Tricare to switch your PCM. The doctor will not be offended; sometimes people just don't click. What's more important is that you are comfortable with your health care provider.

What should you do if Tricare denies your request? This may sound silly, but start by simply hanging up with the bureaucrat you were speaking to, then calling back until you find a sympathetic one. Or go down to the MTF and visit the local Tricare rep. Sometimes the first bureaucrat is someone who is too young or inexperienced to give you a good answer, whether it's the answer you want or an alternative solution to the problem. If working with other Tricare bureaucrats does not solve your problem, call your doctor and ask him to deal with Tricare. He has more clout and can often get the right answers by knowing whom to go to, what logic to use, and which buttons to push.

To get future appointments faster than by calling a hospital's appointment line, ask your doctor at your first meeting if there's an easier way to contact him or her for questions or appointments. Oftentimes, doctors have a nurse or other health care provider who can answer calls quickly and arrange appointments in order to avoid bureaucratic hassles and to provide more personal service.

If you actually call this nurse and she gives you advice instead of allowing you to talk to the doctor, don't assume she is malevolently preventing you from doing so. Instead, she is probably discussing it briefly with the doctor behind the scenes, or perhaps she commonly deals with the situation you are presenting. By running interference for the doctor, she is helping you get advice quickly. Your only other option may be to go through the hassle of making an appointment.

Dealing with a receptionist is a different ball game than

When I was five months pregnant, I moved with my husband to a nine-week training program. Recognizing I would need two visits with the obstetrician during that time, I called up Tricare to relocate my coverage to the new region. Unfortunately, I got a young, burgeoning bureaucrat on the line who had obviously never had a baby. She typed in my zip code and—*voilà!*—pulled up an Air Force hospital located two hours away. When I protested at the ridiculousness of having to travel two hours, particularly if there was an emergency, she insisted that was what the rules said. So I thanked her, went to my appointment, and promptly visited the Tricare office at the hospital to vent my frustration. Sure enough, they agreed with me and gave me permission to see a civilian doctor 15 minutes from my home.

talking to a nurse. Receptionists on the hospital appointment line do not have the training to assess your medical condition, so don't expect them to. They have no medical training and are trained solely to guess whether you need a 15- or 45-minute appointment with the doctor or other health care provider. Thus, you need to communicate exactly that by explaining the depth of your concern. Having said that, don't waste your doctor's time by insisting on a 45-minute visit to address sinus congestion, or go to a 15-minute appointment with a huge list of ailments, or wait until the last minute to raise the real issue concerning you.

Don't be modest with your health care provider, either. Your doctor and health care providers have seen literally thousands of crotches and other private places. Anything you show them they will have seen before. What is more important than your girlish modesty is getting solid health advice. So don't think you're being cute by acting squeamish or making the doctor guess at what's wrong.

If you're not sure whether you should see a health care provider, call the Nurse HelpLine at either your local MTF or through Tricare. This 24/7 hot line is available through the main 1-800 number for your Tricare region listed below.

A final tip is to talk with friends and neighbors about the best care facility in your area. Major military hospitals have some of the world's leading specialists, but you may get lost in the system and have to wait for hours for your appointment. Community hospitals or satellite family clinics are often a good choice for routine care.

TRICARE REGIONS AND CONTACT INFORMATION

Region 1 (Northeast)
★ All of New England south to metropolitan Washington, DC, including Pennsylvania, New Jersey, and Northern Virginia
★ Contractor: Sierra Military Health Services
★ Beneficiary services: 1-888-999-5195
★ Health care finder: 1-888-333-4522
★ Routine claims: 1-800-578-1294

Region 2 (Mid-Atlantic)
★ North Carolina and most of Virginia (except metro Washington, DC)
★ Contractor: Humana Military Healthcare Services
★ 1-800-931-9501

Regions 3 (Southeast) and 4 (Gulf South)
★ Florida, Georgia, South Carolina, Alabama, Tennessee, Mississippi, the eastern third of Louisiana (including New Or-

leans and Baton Rouge), and a small part of Arkansas that's in the Millington, Tennessee, Naval Hospital service area
★ Contractor: Humana Military Healthcare Services
★ Beneficiary services: 1-800-444-5445
★ Health care finder: 1-800-333-4040
★ Routine claims: 1-800-403-3950

Region 5 (Heartland)
★ Michigan, Wisconsin, Illinois, Indiana, Ohio, Kentucky, metropolitan St. Louis, and most of Western Virginia
★ Contractor: Humana Military Healthcare Services
★ 1-800-941-4501

Region 6 (Southwest)
★ Oklahoma, Arkansas (except near Millington, Tennessee), western Louisiana, and most of Texas (except the southwestern part of the state, including El Paso)
★ Contractor: Health Net Federal Services
★ 1-800-406-2832

Central Region (formerly known as Regions 7 and 8)
★ Arizona, Nevada, New Mexico, Colorado, Wyoming, Utah, most of Idaho, Montana, North and South Dakota, Kansas, Nebraska, Minnesota, Iowa, southwestern Texas, and Missouri. Exceptions are metropolitan St. Louis, Missouri; Rock Island, Illinois; and Yuma, Arizona.
★ Contractor: TriWest Health Alliance
★ Beneficiary services and health care finder: 1-888-874-9378
★ Routine claims: 1-877-225-4816

Regions 9 (Southern California) and 10 (Golden Gate)
★ Contractor: Health Net Federal Services
★ Beneficiary services and health care finder: 1-800-242-6788
★ Routine claims: 1-800-930-2929

Region 11 (Northwest)
★ Alaska, Washington, Oregon, and Northern Idaho
★ Contractor: Health Net Federal Services
★ Beneficiary services and health care finder: 1-800-404-2042
★ For Alaska only: beneficiary services and health care finder: 1-800-242-6788; routine claims: 1-800-378-7568

Tricare Pacific
★ Hawaii and Western Pacific
★ 1-800-242-6788

Tricare Europe
★ Europe, Africa, Middle East, Azores, and Iceland
★ 1-888-777-8343

Tricare Latin America/Canada
★ Panama, Central and South America, Puerto Rico, the Virgin Islands, Canada, and the West Indies
★ 1-888-777-8343

DENTAL CARE

Servicemembers receive free dental care through military dentists, and they are required to have regularly scheduled appointments. For families, inexpensive dental insurance using civilian dentists is offered by the military through a contractor, United Concordia (http://www.ucci.com).

There are two plans you can purchase. The single-member plan covers only one dependent and costs just $8.14 per month (per 2003 rates). The family plan covers multiple family members and costs just $20.35 per month. The maximum United Concordia will spend on any enrollee in any fiscal year is $1,200, although certain preventative and diagnostic treatments are not applied against that maximum. Additionally, there is a $1,500 lifetime cap on orthodontia for each enrollee.

★★★ DID YOU KNOW? ★★★

Be aware that there are delays between signing up and actually receiving dental coverage, so don't wait to enroll. You don't want to spend a month in agony with a chipped tooth before you can see a dentist, and you may not receive coverage at that point anyway since the incident happened before you were covered.

Visit http://www.ucci.com to sign up for coverage, which includes automatic enrollment in the Tricare Dental Program (TDP—the overarching government authority) and arranges your monthly payment to be taken by allotment directly from your servicemember's pay.

The Least You Need to Know
★ Military doctors are trained in regular medical schools, but they have special expertise in military-specific needs, such as tropical diseases and biological and chemical warfare.
★ Tricare is just like a regular HMO. You have to work the system in order to reap the benefits, and that means working with your doctor to get the care you need covered by insurance.

Resources
★ http://tma.osd.mil—The Tricare website.
★ Tricare Mail-Order Pharmacy—1-866-363-8667 in the U.S., or 1-866-275-4732 overseas.
★ http://www.ucci.com—United Concordia's website regarding your dental benefits.

Health Care Benefits

9

Relocation and Housing

"**R**elocation" is a scary word for many new military wives and women, but it sometimes means adventure for the more experienced. The first move is always the most difficult because of the stress of moving and learning your way through the bureaucratic process. Every move after that gets easier, and believe it or not, many families turn relocation into a family vacation. If you learn the system and follow the tips and tricks of your fellow wives, you, too, can make relocation easy and even fun.

As stated earlier, the frequency and distance of any relocation depends on your servicemember's career. I'd estimate that 80 percent of military families can predict where they'll be stationed next. For the 20 percent who can't, either they weren't paying attention to the billets at stake or the system had a rare last-minute billet that only your servicemember could fill. Of course, there have also been situations where the servicemember misled his spouse about available billets in order to follow his preferred career track, even though it meant living in a less preferable location. Many hard-core Marines, for example, would love to be stationed in bizarrely remote locations with great operational opportunities, like Twentynine Palms, California, even though their families might go crazy from the heat and lack of civilization.

Whatever your situation, you and your servicemember should be having lengthy discussions about your future at least six months before applying for billets, when your detailer begins to indicate which billets might be available. When it comes time for your servicemember to see the actual list of billets and select his top three or four choices, neither you nor he should be surprised, and he should be able to enter his choices by rote without having to check in with you. This is important in case your servicemember is forced to negotiate with his detailer or with other servicemembers competing for the same billets and cannot call you to discuss the options.

MOVING YOUR HOUSEHOLD GOODS

All relocations are handled by your base Personal Property Office (PPO) of the Traffic Management Office (TMO). Either PPO or TMO may be referred to when base officials talk about who handles your move, so be aware of both acronyms. We'll use "PPO" when discussing this bureaucracy.

Before you freak out over the cost of movers and en route hotels, know that the military is required to pay for moving your family as well as your household goods.

For a Permanent Change of Station (**PCS**) move—typically referred to as "PCSing"—you have three choices on how to move your household goods: commercial movers hired by the military, a do-it-yourself or **DITY** move, or a combination of both, known as a partial DITY move. The first choice is the easiest. Professional movers pack all of your stuff and get it to you within a specific period of time, based on the distance between locations. Believe it or not, they are better than you at packing your wedding china, and they're required to unpack all your stuff upon arrival (although you must put it away). The military will pay for your move only up to a certain weight allowance, which is dependent on your pay grade. Although very few fami-

2003 TABLE OF JOINT FEDERAL TRAVEL REGULATIONS WEIGHT ALLOWANCES*

Grade	PCS Without Dependents	PCS with Dependents	Temporary Allowance
O-10	18,000	18,000	2,000
O-9	18,000	18,000	1,500
O-8	18,000	18,000	1,000
O-7	18,000	18,000	1,000
O-6	18,000	18,000	800
O-5	16,000	17,500	800
O-4/W-4	14,000	17,000	800
O-3/W-3	13,000	14,500	600
O-2/W-2	12,500	13,500	600
O-1/W-1	10,000	12,000	600
E-9	12,000	14,500	600
E-8	11,000	13,500	500
E-7	10,500	12,500	400
E-6	8,000	11,000	400
E-5	7,000	9,000	400
E-4	7,000	8,000	400
E-3	5,000	8,000	400
E-2	5,000	8,000	400
E-1	5,000	8,000	400

*In pounds

Source: Per Diem Committee

lies exceed their weight allowance, it's worth it to throw a pre-move yard sale to avoid paying moving costs for anything above your weight allowance. According to the Department of Defense, a good way to estimate your total weight is to figure 1,000 pounds per room (not including bathrooms), then add that to the estimated weight of appliances and other large items you plan to move.

It is also important to note that the military will not ship any automobiles if you are moving within CONUS, and it will ship only one car if you are moving overseas. As a result, most families relocate within CONUS using two cars. And that makes a DITY or partial DITY more plausible—if not profitable—for families who don't have a lot of furniture to move.

DITY moves are not for the faint of heart or those who tend to be disorganized. Basically, the government estimates its cost to move your household goods, and then pays you 95 percent of that cost to move it yourself. You can get the money in advance so that expenses such as a rental truck and packing materials don't come out of your pocket. The government's estimate is based on the weight of your household goods, not to exceed your weight allowance. Whether you use your car or a rental truck, you will be expected to weigh your empty vehicle in advance and then again when full at an official truck-weighing station in order to determine the weight of your household goods. Those are the same weigh stations you see on the side of the highway with hordes of Mack trucks. The weight cannot include a car in tow. Your PPO counselor will give you more specific details on what is required to certify your weight, but there are definitely a couple of hoops to jump through.

Be careful: If you overestimate the weight during counseling and receive an advance, and then find out you have less weight when you measure it at the truck-weighing station, you will have to pay back the extra amount. Also, be sure to get approval from PPO for a DITY move or you might not get paid or even reimbursed for your expenses. PPO also strongly recommends getting insurance for your rental truck and household goods during shipment. And storage of your DITY-moved goods at your destination may increase your costs; since the government doesn't like to deal with DITY storage, it will reimburse you only for what they would pay at a government facility and does not reimburse for damage that occurs during a DITY storage.

Again, talk to PPO or the relocation counselor at your base Family Support Center to help determine whether a commercial or DITY move—or some combination—is right for you.

Equally important, before you sign up for a DITY move, be sure to call around to find the best price on rental trucks and insurance. You'll find that one-way rentals are astoundingly expensive, and a DITY move may not be as profitable as you think.

REIMBURSEMENT FOR YOUR TRAVEL

The military recognizes that it costs a lot of money to move your family to your new home, so it offers several types of reimbursement. The biggest chunk of change will come from Dislocation Allowance (DLA) to cover the cost of, well, "dislocation" from your current home. Be sure to ask your relocation counselor or Personnel Support Detachment (PSD) for the latest rates since they change from year to year.

Although DLA is generally paid ten days in advance, your DLA may not show up as soon as you need it to begin covering moving expenses. Be sure to nag your servicemember to press his command admin to pay his DLA as soon as possible. The worst-case scenario is that it arrives long after you've maxed out your credit cards with hotel and gas station bills.

In the same lump sum payment with DLA, you will typically receive your Travel Allowance (although you can receive it after you arrive if you don't ask for it early). This is intended to cover your actual travel and food expenses during the trip. It is a combination of the servicemember's Personal Travel Allowance (15 cents per mile plus flat per diem $50) and the Dependent Travel Allowances (17 cents per mile for one dependent; 19 cents per mile for two dependents; 20 cents per mile for more than two dependents). The Travel Allowance also authorizes a per diem of $37.50 for dependents ages 12 and older and a flat rate of $25 per day for ages 12 and under. Mileage and travel time between your current and new home have already been estimated by the Department of Defense, so check with your relocation counselor or PSD to see how much you'll receive. For

DLA RATES FOR 2003

Pay Grade	Without Dependent Rate	With Dependent Rate
O-10	$2,708.27	$3,333.86
O-9	$2,708.27	$3,333.86
O-8	$2,708.27	$3,333.86
O-7	$2,708.27	$3,333.86
O-6	$2,484.63	$3,001.84
O-5	$2,393.02	$2,893.49
O-4	$2,217.65	$2,550.63
O-3	$1,777.27	$2,110.24
O-2	$1,409.79	$1,801.89
O-1	$1,187.15	$1,610.78
O-3E	$1,919.14	$2,267.89
O-2E	$1,631.47	$2,046.23
O-1E	$1,402.90	$1,890.56
W-5	$2,253.11	$2,461.97
W-4	$2,000.90	$2,257.05
W-3	$1,681.72	$2,067.90
W-2	$1,493.54	$1,902.40
W-1	$1,250.18	$1,645.26
E-9	$1,643.30	$2,166.42
E-8	$1,508.31	$1,854.12
E-7	$1,288.62	$1,854.12
E-6	$1,166.44	$1,713.24
E-5	$1,075.82	$1,540.82
E-4	$ 935.92	$1,540.82
E-3	$ 918.18	$1,540.82
E-2	$ 745.78	$1,540.82
E-1	$ 665.01	$1,540.82

Source: Per Diem Committee

overseas rates in particular, visit the Per Diem Committee website at http://www.dtic.mil/perdiem/.

If you are relocating overseas, your personnel office will give your command admin a packet of information and forms to fill out with you, including preferences for travel, which will dictate your DLA and travel pay. Passport forms and other tech-

★★★ **DID YOU KNOW?** ★★★

If you are relocating and hope to move into base housing, plan to live in temporary civilian lodging first. It may take several months before your number comes up on the base housing waiting list. In the meantime, you can either move twice (the second time at your expense) or keep your stuff in storage.

nical problems will also be covered. Never fear! Your command admin will guide you through and help make travel arrangements within your budget, probably via a Space Available flight on a military transport plane.

Temporary Lodging Expenses (TLE) is a little-known authorized pay in addition to your Travel and Dislocation Allowances. It's little known because you have to request it from your command admin, and the paperwork is a bit complicated.

TLE is intended to cover your lodging expenses *once you arrive* at your duty station until you settle into a home. You cannot be paid TLE if you do your house hunting in advance of your PCS. You can receive this pay for up to ten days if your new duty

★★★ **DID YOU KNOW?** ★★★

The government will insist that you pay for relocation expenses on the government-issued credit card as much as possible. As explained in chapter 7, "Personal Finances—Military Style," be very careful to ensure that every cent of your statement is paid in full or you may be reported to your command.

station is CONUS, five days if you are headed overseas. The Per Diem rate, the maximum of which is $110 per day, is based on your travel plans and the Max Locality Rate at your current or future home. If you don't know what that is, it's just another reason to visit your relocation counselor or personnel office to get an estimate. You may also receive an additional flat rate of $37.50 per day if you have dependents over 12 years of age, and $25 per day if you have dependents under 12.

You should arrange for TLE in advance instead of being reimbursed on arrival. Receipts *must* be provided either way, and your mileage must be calculated, which is why most people don't bother with TLE. Without receipts, *the military will force you to pay back TLE by withholding your servicemember's pay.* In addition, you cannot receive TLE for your first or last PCS. The government figures it doesn't owe you for that.

Finally, the military will give you an advance on your Basic Allowance for Housing (BAH) *as a loan* to cover the costs of moving in, such as deposits on a new apartment and utilities (not government housing). You then pay back this interest-free loan over 12 months through an allotment. See your command admin for more information. Our advice is to get advance BAH to cover deposits on your new location, but pay it back immediately upon receiving your security deposits back from the old location.

★★★ DID YOU KNOW? ★★★

Security deposits on utilities can get expensive! You may be able to avoid them by asking your current utility company to send you letters of reference for your new utility company to review when setting up an account.

HOUSE-HUNTING LEAVE

According to DoD regulations, your servicemember is authorized to take up to ten days of house-hunting leave, and even more for a PCS overseas. This time off is in addition to regular vacation and travel time between bases. However, not all commands authorize house-hunting leave if things are too hectic to allow time off, so be sure to have your servicemember check with his new command. Sometimes it is better to take house-hunting leave a few months before moving in order to secure a place to live immediately upon arrival. In such cases, time will be taken away from and must be authorized by the old command. More frequently, a new command will allow the servicemember to tack on the ten days of house-hunting leave to his travel time, even if he has already found a place to live.

Please note that if you opt to house hunt upon arrival at your new CONUS duty station, you can receive the TLE allowance—but not if you opt to house hunt before you relocate. You will have to bear the expense of travel and lodging. Overseas house hunting is different, and it is possible to receive TLE for it.

Also, family members' travel expenses may not be covered by TLE during house hunting, with one exception: One family member may travel overseas on military transport (known as "Space A") for house-hunting purposes, if the travel takes place in advance of the PCS. Obviously, you can house hunt with your servicemember within CONUS, but you will have to cover your own expenses.

This is admittedly all very confusing. If I am boring you by repeating the need to visit your relocation counselor, personnel office, and PPO, be assured that they can tie up all of the above details into one basic estimate for your total cost of moving and reimbursement. You'll feel much more in control of your finances—and moving options—when you receive your individualized relocation estimates. The report below, for example, provides a Navy E-5 the exact info he needs to move his household goods (estimated weight, the maximum 9,000 lbs.) and family from Groton, Connecticut, to San Diego, California:

ESTIMATE:

Travel Advance:	**$3,777.30**
Net Due at Claim Liquidation:	**$815.86**

Net Payment:	**$4,593.16**

BASED ON:

Origination:	**GROTON, CT**	Move Type:	**PERMANENT**
Destination:	**SAN DIEGO, CA**	Estimated Weight:	**9,000**
Distance:	**2,877 miles**	Max Weight Allowed:	**9,000**
Paygrade:	**E-5**	Government Cost:	**$6,295.50**
Dependents:	**YES**	MRT:	**$59.95**

CALCULATION EXPLANATION:

Government Cost x 60% = Travel Advance:	**$3,777.30**
Government Cost x 95% = Member Entitlement (estimate for a DITY move):	**$5,980.73**
Member Entitlement x 27.5% = Federal Tax: (see **Note**)	**$1,387.57**
Member Entitlement – Travel Advance – Federal Tax = Net Due at Claim Liquidation:	**$815.86**
Travel Advance + Net Due at Claim Liquidation = Net Payment:	**$4,593.16**

Note: The taxable portion of the Member Entitlement is reduced by providing receipts for allowable deductions, such as the cost of a rental vehicle, packing materials, moving aids, tolls, and gas.

Source: Naval Supply Systems Command Household Goods website at http://www.smartwebmove.navsup.navy.mil

THE LOGISTICAL PROCESS OF
MOVING WITH THE MILITARY

Legally speaking, spouses are not authorized to work with PPO to move household goods unless you have a specific Power of Attorney (POA) from the base legal office. PPO will tell you that's because the military is really paying for the servicemember's move, not yours, even if 95 percent of the "household goods" is your stuff. Yes, you are chopped liver in their eyes.

The real story, however, is that a handful of military wives took advantage of PPO in the past to move their household goods to a new location when the servicemember had no orders to move or was moving to a different location. In other words, these ladies got PPO to help them leave their husbands. How they got away with it, I don't know, because PPO requires you to show proof of orders to relocate before they'll even discuss relocation with you. And you can't relocate to a household that is more than 50 miles from your new command. Even so, these

★★★ **DID YOU KNOW?** ★★★

Even though most base legal offices can get you a POA within ten minutes without an appointment, relying on your servicemember to deal with PPO is not a bad idea, even if you are a complete control freak. Surprisingly, there are only about two forms to fill out, both of which require his signature anyway, and the only thing PPO wants to know is when you want your stuff packed up and when you want it delivered. PPO may make your servicemember sit through a mind-numbing one-hour class on how to move, but he's used to these types of lectures by now, and some of the information can be quite helpful.

ladies' stories made for terrific mythology within the PPO bureaucracy, and now the rest of us are forced to rely on our servicemember or get a POA.

Within a week or so of submitting the requisite paperwork and proof of orders to PPO, you should receive a response telling you which moving company has been hired, when they will arrive, and approximately when they will deliver your stuff at your new location. The sooner you submit this paperwork and get the process going, the more likely you will be moved on the preferred dates you indicated.

STORAGE

The military generally does not like to deal with storage, but you are entitled to up to 90 days of temporary storage at origin, en route, or at the final destination during any PCS move. Extensions are possible, as is permanent storage in certain circumstances, so talk to your PPO counselor.

You can also have movers pick up your household goods from storage, but PPO warns that you are required to meet the movers at the storage facility and unpack your goods so they can repack and load them professionally.

Relocation and Housing

SHIPPING YOUR CARS

Servicemembers are currently entitled to have only one car (referred to as a Personally Owned Vehicle or **POV**) shipped if they are moving overseas. The military will not ship cars for a move within CONUS. There is some discussion of changing this policy because of the dangerousness of families driving two cars cross-country, and to reflect the needs of modern families. The military will ship motorcycles as part of your household weight allowance.

For overseas relocation, many families opt not to ship their car because: 1) you must first drop it off at a military car-shipment port, which may be hundreds of miles away; 2) it takes forever (90 days) for the vehicle to arrive; and 3) American cars often are not permitted to operate in the destination country or at least do not fit in well. SUVs are particularly difficult to drive on the narrow roads of many foreign countries. Also, in many foreign countries cars are driven on the left-hand side of the road, instead of the right-hand side as in America. For this reason, American cars with the driver's seat on the left side make it confusing and even dangerous to drive in other countries. Better to arrive, drive a rental car for a bit to familiarize yourself, and then buy a car locally. You can have it shipped back to the United States upon your return if you wish, but many families just sell it.

★★★ DID YOU KNOW? ★★★

Unless you have a reason to be concerned about both adults driving, I recommend getting a cheap walkie-talkie system and driving both cars. You'll save a ton of money and still be able to chatter all the way.

For moves within CONUS, some families opt to have their vehicle shipped at their own expense. The cost is typically around $1,000 for a cross-country move, and you can receive your car usually within 15 days or so. Obviously, this is an additional expense, but it is an alternative for families who worry about both parents driving simultaneously across country or who want to turn their trip into a family vacation.

SHIPPING A MOBILE HOME

A mobile home may be shipped at government expense if you are PCSing within the United States or overseas, so long as you plan to use it as a residence. Temporary storage (90 days) is approved but may not be available in your location. This is one time when it may pay for you to do a DITY move of your home instead of having the government move your home for you. Again, check with PPO regarding your entitlements.

SHIPPING YOUR BOAT

Amazingly, the military will ship a boat with a length of 14 feet or less. Basically, you get to include the weight of your boat in the weight allowance for all your household goods, although if it exceeds 14 feet you will have to ship it in a separate container at your own expense. If you are traveling overseas, and your boat fits into a standard container despite being over 14 feet, you're covered. You may also sail your boat to your new destination and be reimbursed for your expenses upon arrival. Houseboats are treated in the same way as mobile homes.

SHIPPING FIREARMS

The shipment of firearms is probably the last thing you're concerned about during your move, but your servicemember probably owns at least one and there are regulations involved. If the movers will not pack them for you, you may have to travel with your firearms in your baggage. That means you must pack them appropriately (i.e., dismantled and unloaded) and carry your registration with you. It is also important to have your military I.D. and orders in hand because some states and countries prohibit some types of firearms unless owned by a military servicemember. When traveling with firearms to and from overseas locales, be sure to declare them on your customs forms in order to prevent an international incident. It would not be pleasant for friends and family to see your face on CNN as a detained alleged terrorist.

RELOCATING PETS

The first thing you need to relocate your pet is a recent health certificate (within 20 days of travel) from your current veterinarian stating that your pet is healthy and up-to-date on its vaccinations. While this is not as critical when moving within CONUS, it is absolutely critical when moving overseas. Because of the incidence of rabies within the United States, many foreign countries and the state of Hawaii require certification of rabies vaccination and may still quarantine your pet for 30 days or longer. Most countries also charge a pet entrance fee and may restrict certain exotic pets and dog breeds, namely pit bull terriers. For details on your destination, talk to your relocation counselor at the Family Support Center, and check with the consulate of your host country before trying to ship a pet.

When traveling with pets within CONUS, most families

carry the pet in the car using a pet carrier and make plenty of bathroom stops. Be sure to make your travel plans in advance, as most hotels do not accept pets. The only exception is La Quinta Inns (1-800-531-5900), which accept up to two 40-pound, well-behaved pets at all of their locations. (God bless them!)

When relocating pets overseas, you should be able to fly them with you whether you are traveling by commercial or military aircraft. However, be sure to check the rules before assuming your pets are okay to go.

TRAVELING OVERSEAS

The main thing to know about traveling overseas is that it just takes longer to receive your household goods. For that reason, the military typically pays for a temporary rental car and permits a small shipment of "unaccompanied baggage"—i.e., stuff you will need immediately upon arrival while waiting for your main shipment of household goods. Unaccompanied baggage is packed and shipped separately from your household goods and usually includes items such as kitchen utensils and dishes, daily-use linens, and baby cribs. Your relocation counselor can help you determine your unaccompanied baggage entitlement, but below is a table of weight allowances to help you get started.

Army Unaccompanied Baggage Allowances

Military Members on Permanent Change of Station	Allowance Pounds
General Officers (0–8, 0–9, 0–10)	1,000
General Officers (0–7) and Colonels (0–6)	800
Other officers	600
Enlisted members	500

Dependents of Military Members

Each adult and child 12 years and older	350
Each child under 12 years of age	175

Air Force Unaccompanied Baggage Allowances

If grade is	and member is	then allowance is
0–1 to 0–5	PCS	600 lb. net weight *(see notes 1 & 2)*
0–6	PCS	800 lb. net weight *(see notes 1 & 2)*
0–7 to 0–10	PCS	1,000 lb. net weight *(see notes 1 & 2)*
E-1 to E-9	PCS serving unaccompanied tour overseas	500 lb. net weight *(see notes 1 & 2)*
E-1 to E-9	PCS serving accompanied tour overseas	400 lb. net weight *(see note 1)*
E-1 to E-9	PCS within CONUS	400 lb. net weight
E-1 to 0-10	PCS and authorized movement of dependents	350 lb. net weight for each dependent 12 yrs. or older; 175 lb. net weight for dependents less than 12 yrs. old

Notes: 1) Single and unaccompanied members assigned to duty stations outside the continental United States have two options. They may ship the normal allowance or 10 percent of their full weight allowance by surface (700 lbs. for E-1 through E-4, with two years or less). This surface option is also authorized for the member of a military couple not authorized household goods allowance. When the member elects surface option, the shipment may include household goods. Split shipments (part by air, part by surface) are not authorized. 2) For unaccompanied members assigned to hardlift areas, shipment of the 10 percent option by air is authorized.

Navy, Marine Corps, and Coast Guard Unaccompanied Baggage Allowances

Navy, Marine Corps, and Coast Guard members should contact their respective transportation offices for unaccompanied baggage allowances.

Source: Joint Travel Regulations

MOVING OUT

If you plan to have the military handle your move, the moving company will probably call you to set up a pre-move meeting, in which they review your household to get an idea of how much weight and bulk they will have to pack. They have no restrictions on dealing with spouses, so now you can take back control of your move. This is a good opportunity to assess the professionalism of your mover, get contact phone and cell phone numbers, and find out how long the process will take. If you have any concerns about your mover, or hear something bad through the grapevine, call PPO immediately and ask to be assigned to a different company. You may not be moved on the dates you preferred, and the PPO bureaucrat may give you a bit of a hassle, but at least your stuff will arrive intact. The military gives most movers up to two days to pack your house, one day for packing and one day for loading, and most movers will use up all of that time in order to be paid the highest rate.

The week before your move, you will start to get anxious and try to pre-pack things. Don't. Instead, try to focus your energy on saying good-bye to old friends. The two to three days before your move, however, there are several things you can do to get organized for the big day:

★ If moving overseas, separate your unaccompanied baggage from your main shipment of household goods.

★ Give away your household plants to friends and neighbors, and wash out any good pots you wish to keep.

★ Disconnect all household appliances you intend to ship, and defrost the refrigerator at least 24 hours in advance.

★ If shipping machines such as a motorcycle or lawn mower, remove any gasoline or oil from the engine.

★ Clean out your garage of anything the movers are unlikely to pack and that you probably won't use in the future, such as paint, aerosols, and cleansers.

★ Back up important files on your computer to a CD-ROM or diskette, and plan to take it with you.

★ Record the serial numbers and, if possible, take photos of any expensive electronics equipment or furniture. This prevents a disreputable mover from attempting to deliver a 20-year-old clunker TV instead of the brand-new flat screen you actually own.

★ Separate the servicemember's professional goods, such as books or equipment, from the rest of the household. The movers should weigh them separately because they will not count against your weight allowance.

★ Dismantle anything with electrical cords, such as computers, televisions, and stereos.

★ Purchase food and drinks for yourself and the movers, such as sodas, donuts, and granola bars. Plan to buy your movers lunch. Bribery and goodwill are everything to your movers!

★ Arrange for day care and pet care if possible. Kids and pets tend to get in the way and create safety hazards, and just watching the move will unnecessarily stress them out.

★ Empty your trash can and put out a large trash bag with a big sign that says TRASH. Otherwise, the movers will pack your full trash can, which you will discover weeks later when you unpack.

★ If you are driving two cars, invest in walkie-talkies for the trip. It makes driving safer and more fun.

★ Consider investing in an overhead travel compartment that is secured on top of your car. It clears out space inside the car, making travel safer and more comfortable, and you'll use it for years to come.

You will also need to set aside items you want to take with your family while you travel. I strongly recommend putting all of these items in your car the night before to ensure they fit reasonably comfortably and so the movers don't accidentally pack them. These items include:

★ Packed suitcases for the entire family.

★ Important files, such as your servicemember's orders and service records, the household inventory list the movers will provide you, serial numbers and photos of any expensive equipment and furniture, car ownership and insurance papers, and Tricare insurance cards and phone numbers. You should also include CD-ROMs containing the backed-up files from your computer.

★ Expensive jewelry and other family heirlooms. Pack these at the bottom of your car where gas station thieves cannot quickly get to them.

★ Travel toys for the kids.

★ Snack foods for the trip.

★ Paper plates, cups, and plastic utensils to use while living in an empty house. You may be too tired or forget to buy them when you arrive. Later on, this will save money and calories from eating out.

★ Extra bath towels.

★ Blankets and pillows to sleep on after the movers pack your bed and in case you have a few nights in your new home before they arrive.

★ A small tool kit containing duct tape, a hammer, a four-headed screwdriver, and pliers.

★ A laundry basket in which you will ultimately place all items the movers cannot pack, such as detergents, cosmetics, and aerosols. These items cost a lot when added together, and you'll need these anyway when you arrive at your new location and have an amazing urge to clean. Include in the laundry basket several rolls of toilet paper and paper towels because you'll be too tired to do a grocery run when you first arrive. You can place the extra towels over the basket to keep things cool and prevent spills.

★ Pet needs.

★ Your walkie-talkies and cell phones.

If you plan to do a DITY or partial DITY move, you obviously want to call around to find the best price on a rental truck, assuming you need one. Be sure to do that months in advance to avoid the relocation stampede and ensure you get access to a truck when you need it. Otherwise, you are solely responsible for getting your stuff to the new location, and the military will accept no excuses for arriving late.

The anticipation of moving day is often worse than moving day itself. If professional movers are handling your move, you want to set aside a book to read or change-of-address cards to write because you'll have hours with nothing to do. Not only do you not have to pack anything, they won't let you for liability reasons!

Better yet, spend your time paying close attention to the Household Goods Descriptive Inventory list. The mover will tag every box or piece of furniture with a small sticker with a number on it. The mover-in-chief will subsequently record the tag number and the box's contents on the inventory list as it is being loaded onto the truck. It's important that every item is accounted for, because your stuff will be placed on a truck with at least one other shipment of household goods, and then it may be shipped, stored, and handled multiple times by the movers before arriving at the final destination. I don't care what PPO or the movers say: Your stuff will be double- or triple-handled by your definition. That means it will be loaded onto a Mack truck, unloaded into a local storage unit, reloaded onto another truck for travel, unloaded at a second storage unit in your new hometown, and finally reloaded and delivered to your new doorstep. If you don't pay attention to the inventory list at both ends of your move, you increase the chance of boxes and furniture getting lost.

You will be asked to sign two other forms in addition to the Household Goods Descriptive Inventory, and you should receive copies of all three. DD Form 619 lists the number of boxes and weight of your shipment, so use it to make sure you have not gone over your weight allowance. The Government Bill of Lading describes approximately when the shipment will arrive at its destination and who your point of contact is.

If you're doing a DITY move, plan for some serious physical labor and take time-outs to reenergize with food and rest.

Either way, expect to be exhausted and without a television or bed the night after moving day. If you're lucky, the movers may finish early and you can start your trip to the new base. More likely, however, you're better off enjoying an easygoing

---

★★★ DID YOU KNOW? ★★★

Serious control freaks who are worried about losing their stuff go so far as to print out their own paper labels with their family's name and contact information and place one on each item. This way, other families who have received a stray box can call you and have it shipped.

evening at your favorite restaurant and going to bed early on your makeshift bed. You have a long trip ahead!

THE BIG TRIP

Traveling with the family can be really fun! You're done with your move and free of responsibilities, so why not enjoy the scenery together? Like any family vacation, the key is to recognize family preferences and plan ahead. For example, if you are traveling by car across the country with children and pets, try to plan one outdoor excursion each day. You'll get to stretch your legs and see America's great national parks. Having said that, after a week or two of traveling, you and your family will have had enough and want nothing more than to settle in and eat a home-cooked meal. Plan for these preferences—and for contingencies—in order to avoid excessive tension during your trip.

If you are traveling overseas, most of your trip will be planned through your command admin, relocation counselor, and PPO, so you shouldn't have too much to worry about other than marking off each item on your bureaucratic to-do checklist. Once you're on the plane, however, you're free to relax and dream about future adventures—so long as you've brought the requisite snacks and toys to keep you and your family occupied during the long flight.

MOVING IN

Once you and your family arrive at your new location, notify PPO of your arrival and expect to hang out in an empty house for a few days. Movers rarely arrive exactly when they plan to, but will usually show up a day or so later. Getting a cell phone number of the company and/or driver is the best way to keep

★★★ WAR STORIES ★★★
Turning Relocation into a Family Vacation

When my husband and I did our first move together from Washington, DC, to San Diego, we saw it as a tremendous opportunity to spend ten days together and see the country. With our two dogs in tow, we knew our daily drive time would be limited and there would be no way to visit any indoor tourist attractions. We opted to spend the first day driving as far as possible just to get the trip moving. We ended up in Nashville and stayed at a La Quinta Inn near the airport with a huge field to play ball in. The next day, we detoured from the freeway and traveled the Natchez Trace and then west to Shiloh National Military Park. After spending several hours walking with the dogs through that historic landmark, we hit the back roads and drove over the Mississippi River, on into Little Rock, Arkansas.

The next morning we ate a Southern-fried breakfast and headed west into the Ozark Mountains through more back roads, trying to see the legendary land of the Hatfields and McCoys. By Oklahoma City, we had picked up old Route 66 and then toured the famous sites along it, including Cadillac Ranch, and spent the night in Amarillo, Texas. The next day was a short drive to Albuquerque for a visit with old friends, followed by a detour through the old mining town and ski resort of Durango, Colorado, the Mesa Verde cliff dwellings (another national park), an Indian fry bread stand at Four Corners, and the Painted Desert of Arizona. After two nights with family, we completed our journey to San Diego with several days to spare.

We had so much fun, we're planning our next cross-country trip across the northern United States so we can see Yellowstone National Park, the site of Custer's Last Stand, Mount Rushmore, and other sites along the Lewis and Clark trail.

track of your shipment and plan. In the meantime, use the time to clean, line shelves with contact paper, and figure out where you want to place furniture and storage.

Moving in is more intensive than moving out. At this point, your goal is to get settled in as soon as possible. Why? Your family will be absolutely sick of traveling, and it's amazing how the stress disappears once you've reestablished familiar surroundings. Also, at this point you will probably have used up your DLA funds and/or Travel Allowance, and eating out is getting very expensive, not to mention calorie-laden.

The biggest mistake military families make is to let the movers leave without unpacking, which the military is *paying* them to do. The family is then overwhelmed with rooms full of boxes, having no idea which box contains what (even though each box is marked by room) and no way to dispose of the boxes. My girlfriend Robyne spent two months unpacking when she fell for an old movers' trick. The movers harassed her about having to unpack, and then dumped a box of medicine on the floor, where it spilled on the carpet. Frustrated, Robyne ordered them to stop and waived her right to have them unpack.

By contrast, experienced military families can have nearly their entire household unpacked—including pictures on the walls—within four days. Do not use this as your yardstick for success, however, especially on your first move. Just understand that the key to getting unpacked is having an efficient system whereby the movers systematically unpack room by room. As they put something down, you or someone in your family needs

★★★ **DID YOU KNOW?** ★★★

Superefficient control freaks label all their storage cabinets and drawers with Post-it notes in advance so movers themselves can place every item exactly where it needs to go.

to pick it up and put it away. You will know approximately where to put it because you've reviewed your house the night before and gotten a good idea of where things should go.

Don't worry about getting everything exactly right. You can rearrange things later on, once you've had a chance to live in your new home and establish new routines. Far more important is clearing a space for the movers to unpack the next item, and the next. If they run out of space on the countertops or floor, the movers will claim they can no longer unpack and you will be left to fend for yourself.

What should my girlfriend Robyne have done after the unprofessional behavior of her movers? Be professional instead: Insist that they clean up the mess and tell them you expect them to be more professional and careful. If that doesn't work, call PPO immediately to report the problem or, if it's after office hours, call the base Inspector General. Either one is required to come to your home immediately, referee the dispute, and make sure your household items are unpacked safely and professionally. Do not attempt to handle the situation yourself, and do not be intimidated by the movers or worry they will harm your stuff. PPO's job is to make sure your rights to a professional move are not violated.

Of course, it does help to make friends with the movers. Again, you want to start moving-in day by introducing yourself,

Relocation and Housing

walking the movers through the house, and pointing out where you want things. Tell them outright that you expect everything to be unpacked by the end of the day, and then tell them where they can find food and drinks. Buy them lunch at midday and turn on the radio to a station *they* want to listen to. It makes them happy and the day go faster.

The second biggest mistake military families make is not paying close attention when checking off the inventory list and filing claims for lost or damaged goods. Hopefully, you made sure on moving-out day that all of your boxes and furniture were appropriately tagged and listed on the inventory list. Now you will be asked to check off each item as it is unloaded from the truck. This is also a good time to direct movers as to what boxes go to which room. Any items that do not arrive with your shipment or are damaged should be immediately recorded on the mover's paperwork for PPO, DD Form 1840, a pink copy of which you are entitled to receive. Simultaneously, ask the mover to simply check back at his warehouse for the stray item.

After you've signed DD Form 1840 acknowledging any lost or damaged items, the mover will send a copy to PPO, and you will have 70 days to report any additional lost or damaged items and two years to file the completed claim. Be sure to report everything. Not only will you be reimbursed for the cost of your lost items, but it helps PPO identify and impose quality controls on the movers they hire. Having photos and serial numbers on hand will help you process your claim more quickly and be reimbursed the full amount.

Finally, the movers are required by the military to leave with any unpacked boxes. This is critical, because you may have difficulty disposing of them otherwise and they take up a substantial amount of room. Many local garbage companies will not pick up boxes, and it is illegal to dump them in most commercial Dumpsters.

HOUSING

You have two options for housing: government-subsidized housing typically located on a military base, or regular civilian housing. "Housing" refers not only to homes but also apartments, condos, mobile homes, and even houseboats. As a point of reference, within CONUS only 10 to 20 percent of military families live on base, while 80 to 90 percent live in civilian housing. Overseas, the reverse is more often the case.

The decision to live in base housing within CONUS is usually determined by personal preference, local cost of living, the quality of housing, and the "pain in the butt" factor involved in dealing with housing bureaucrats. First, personal preferences in housing often involve whether you don't mind living near your servicemember's colleagues and families, or whether you would prefer to put some distance between your family and your husband's work life. Sure, base housing is wonderfully Cleaveresque and safe (think kids playing baseball in the street), and it cuts down on your servicemember's commute time, but you may also have to put up with gossipy neighbors.

The second issue is that, while those living in civilian housing receive a Basic Allowance for Housing (BAH), it may not be enough to cover rent in high-cost areas such as Washington, DC. Many junior enlisted families opt for base housing because, although they lose their BAH payment, they often get a much bigger house and yard, and at no cost. The same size house in a civilian neighborhood would cost them hundreds of dollars extra out of their own pockets.

With regard to the third issue, I won't kid you that much of the current stock of base housing is dilapidated and bug-infested. One neighborhood I know of was actually condemned by the county building inspector, even though the military still attempted to foist it on families. The good news is that the government is on a major campaign to rebuild base housing using private contractors, and overseas housing can be downright posh. Some people are nervous about new restrictions these private contractors may put on families, such as limiting pets or actually making you clean your house, but overall, this will increase standards and quality for base housing.

Finally, there is no denying that dealing with the base Housing Office within CONUS can be a bureaucratic nightmare. To start, you must apply to be on a waiting list for housing, and you can only apply for housing that is designated for your pay grade, even if it is 30 miles from civilization. Even worse, most Housing Offices will not allow you to apply to be on the housing wait list until after you have PCS'd to the area. Thus, even if you are living in Germany and can fax your orders to move to Fort Campbell, Kentucky, as proof that you will be relocating, the Fort Campbell Housing Office will not put you on the waiting list. Amazingly, these very same bureaucrats are shocked—shocked!—when families show up on their doorstep and have no place to live. No, you are responsible for finding temporary housing until it's your turn to be assigned base housing. That could be months or even years depending on your base, and don't be surprised if your number on the wait list gets bumped by families with higher rank or special circumstances.

If you intend to pursue base housing, be sure to read any rental agreement you sign for temporary civilian housing carefully, because you could lose thousands if you attempt to break your rental agreement early. While most rentals near military bases have a "military contingency" clause, a closer inspection will show that you can break your rental agreement only if you have PCS orders to relocate more than 50 miles away. Getting into base housing does not count.

The base Housing Office will insist that you report to it even if you intend from the start to live in civilian housing. Well, no one I know has been flogged for not reporting, although single junior enlisted servicemembers are typically required to live on base and therefore check in with the Housing Office. However, the Housing Office usually has lists of military-friendly apartment complexes and house rental notices. Better yet, if

Warning: Before signing up for a waiting list for a specific neighborhood, be sure to check out the neighborhood, visit with the residents, and travel the distance between it and other important locations such as shopping, work, and day care. Some housing developments are so remote they don't have cell phone coverage. The residents will be happy to tell you everything you need to know because they wish they had had the same advice when they applied for housing. There's no sense in going through the bureaucracy and getting on a waiting list if you will ultimately refuse to live in the dumpy neighborhood.

you want to live in one of these complexes, the Housing Office can usually set you up with a deal to forgo any security deposits, so long as you agree to pay rent by allotment (i.e., directly from your servicemember's pay and deducted from his paycheck).

The logistical process for obtaining one of these deals or getting on the waiting list is simple: Visit your local base Housing Office. Typically, there is no need for an appointment, although you may want to make one if you need help during peak relocation season. A counselor will be assigned to you and will review your options.

You can ignore most of this advice if you are relocating overseas. Overseas base Housing Offices are typically much more flexible because they have to be and they have more housing to accommodate more families. Your relocation counselor can help put you in contact with the Housing Office counselor at your destination base, or see the SITES brochure or website for contact information.

Finally, if you are researching the base and civilian housing

Relocation and Housing

The military's Sponsorship Program pairs relocating service-members with servicemembers already established at the base, usually a future colleague in the new command. The sponsor and his spouse can answer questions and help the re-locating family get established in their new community, and overseas sponsors go so far as to help with travel and logisti-cal arrangements. Really great sponsors will even take you out to dinner and introduce you to their friends. Ask your new command or check your servicemember's orders for informa-tion on how to be paired with a sponsor. Knowing how tough it is to relocate, sign up yourself to become a sponsor and help another family with their move.

at your destination base, be sure to ask the opinion of women who already live there. By simply posting a question on the dis-cussion forums of *CinC*House.com, you can often find a gold mine of answers not mentioned in the official relocation propa-ganda provided to you by your relocation counselor or on SITES. *This* is exactly how you will find out which neighbor-hoods are termite-infested and which are positively opulent.

EASING THE TRANSITION
TO A NEW COMMUNITY

As if moving isn't difficult enough, now you have to help your family settle into a new community. The best thing to do is re-search in advance as much as possible about local jobs, schools, community activities, and neighborhoods. By doing this re-search and keeping your family informed of your findings, you will help them adjust their expectations and get excited before you pack your bags.

Getting the kids settled may be the most difficult task. If you're lucky, the kids will start school a month or so after you arrive. This will allow them to get settled in but not be too bored or lonely. If like most families you arrive at the beginning of summer, it is critical to get the kids signed up for as many activities as possible, especially on base. This allows them to meet new friends and realize that they are not the only kids who have gone through this ordeal. An additional benefit of your kids' finding new friends is that you may meet their parents and make new friends yourself!

Understand that when it comes to settling your family in the community, your example will lead the way. Your kids don't know how to get involved in the community, and your servicemember may be too busy trying to get settled in his job. Yet you know that new friendships and community support are the key to alleviating your family's transition stress. What can you do? Sign up for community activities such as the PTA and spouse club. Throw a party for your neighbors to get to know them better. Go to your servicemember's Hail and Farewell command party to get to know his colleagues and their spouses. Above all, don't let exhaustion and stress get to you. Sitting on the couch does not introduce you to new friends.

Preparing yourself and your family for living overseas is a different ball game because of culture shock. Many naïve people will tell you to "live like the natives" entirely and forgo anything American. Bullfeathers! That approach only works for one-week vacations, not living semipermanently in a foreign country. While you can learn to appreciate other cultures and get your family excited about seeing the world, you cannot change who you are—and you are Americans! You will discover how unique that is when you arrive at your new destination. So plan to visit local historical sites, eat the food, and learn the language. But don't be embarrassed to fall back on the tight-knit community of American expats when the foreign country becomes too much to take.

For those who will live in a foreign country where there is no military base nearby, my father has some great advice he learned while stationed in Korea: When you can't take any more, spend a few hours at the nearest, most American hotel you can find. Even if you can afford only a cup of coffee, it will remind you who you are and reenergize you to face life in a foreign country.

Culture shock is more than just American vs. foreign ways of living. It can also involve severe differences in living standards. If you are moving to a lower-income area, the good news is you can probably afford a fabulous house, maid, and maybe even a nanny! Many a wife who has spent time in Bahrain, for example, has marveled at the palaces and house staff regular military folks acquire upon arrival. Even so, that can protect you only so much from the beggars and squalor often just outside the gates. Again, don't be embarrassed to take a break and fall back on the American expat community. In fact, this is one of the main reasons why the Exchanges operate extensive American-style department stores overseas. Somehow, Tommy Hilfiger fashions and peanut butter make it all feel better. Also, if you or your family is having problems adjusting to your new home, talk to other families about how they deal with culture shock.

PEARLS OF WISDOM FOR A GREAT MOVE

This chapter attempts to give you all the facts about relocation so you can take control of your destiny. Some things, however, will go out of control. Below are some pearls of wisdom from my girlfriend Dawna and numerous *CinC*House gals who have learned from experience:

★ Whatever nasty things are said in the six months surrounding a move should not be held against that person and do not reflect on the state of your marriage.

★ No matter how hard you try, some of your valuables will be lost or damaged during a move. Be grateful your family members are safe and take revenge on the movers by pursuing full reimbursement through PPO and the claims section of the base legal office.

★ When in doubt about your movers, call PPO or the Government Inspector's Office. Do not allow yourself to argue with your movers or travel people. PPO will send someone immediately to mediate between you and the service providers and ensure your family is taken care of.

In addition to the week of and moving-out-day checklists on pages 126–28, use this master checklist as you count down to relocation.

MASTER RELOCATION CHECKLIST

Weeks to Go	Task
12	Upon receiving orders, contact PPO and schedule counseling session to submit paperwork.
12	Meet with relocation counselor at FSC to get an estimate of how much DLA and Travel Allowance you will receive. Begin to plot a budget and time line for travel.
12	Set up a file to track moving and house-

hunting expenses. Whatever is not covered by allowances is tax deductible.

12	Identify your sponsor at your new command who will answer your questions. Begin researching housing and schools in your new city. If you need child care, search for this now.
12	If you own your home and wish to sell, contact a Realtor to put it on the market immediately. If necessary, negotiate with potential buyers to stay in your home until moving-out day.
11	Make an inventory and take pictures of your household possessions and valuables. Send pictures to homeowners/renters insurance company.
11	Meet with PPO to submit paperwork and provide an estimated weight of your household goods. If you go over your weight allowance, get an estimate from movers to pay for the extra amount and begin saving now.
10	Receive moving dates from PPO. Call movers to schedule a pre-move meeting. If doing a DITY move, reserve a rental truck.
9	Compile and update your résumé. Determine the best time to quit your current job. If you can, start the job search now.
9	Review family records (legal, medical, insurance, birth certificates) and set aside in a file. Get checkups if needed and obtain copies of your medical records.
9	Check homeowners/renters and automobile insurance to notify of change of address and make sure you are covered in transit.

9	Make sure your bank is located in your new hometown or sign up with a national bank.
8	Clean out your closets and garage. Hold a yard sale or donate items for the tax deduction.
8	Hopefully you have narrowed down which neighborhoods you want to live in. If you plan to live off base, go house hunting now and try to sign a rental contract. If you plan to live on base, contact the Housing Office and ask if you can sign up for the waiting list— just in case they're easygoing.
7	Check school schedules and transfer kids' records.
7	Have fun planning your travel. Turn it into a vacation.
6	Give one month's notice to employer, get a letter of referral, and use the remaining two weeks to plan your move. Begin full-scale job search.
5	Notify your landlord as required by lease. Discuss a time to review your home and get a refund of your security deposit.
5	Drop-dead date for getting housing in your new hometown because current renters will be giving one-month notice.
4	Obtain a change-of-address kit from the post office. Send change-of-address cards to family, friends, and businesses such as your accountant, magazines to which you subscribe, and so forth.
3	While paying your bills, contact utility companies to cut off service and obtain letters of referral. Notify them of forwarding

	address to receive final bills and refunds of any security deposits. Get a list of utilities in your new hometown from your landlord or real estate agent, and contact them to set up service.
3	Re-verify schedule with PPO and movers.
3	Take the pets to the vet and obtain health certifications and medical records.
2	Make reservations for overnight stays during your last night in town and, if appropriate, for your travel.
2	If you are driving, have your car serviced.
2	If you are shipping your car, have it picked up.
1	Notify credit card companies of change of address. You'll need to use the new address when verifying any purchases.
1	Review checklists for final week and moving day, beginning on page 126.

The Least You Need to Know

★ You will survive relocation no matter where you're planning to move! The military hires professional movers and pays your travel expenses. If you're moving overseas, it will arrange travel for you. Your job is to meet with PPO and the FSC relocation counselor to watch your budget and learn the rules.

★ If you get smart about relocation, you can actually make money and have a terrific family vacation!

★ Base housing is harder to come by than you think. If you wish to live on base, contact the Housing Office as soon as you receive orders. You may have to arrange temporary lodging until your number comes up on the waiting list.

★ Planning ahead and quickly getting settled in your new community will save you and your family a lot of stress.

Resources

★ http://www.cinchouse.com—Visit the Relocation Section for personalized checklists and resources on everything you need to relocate, including finding housing and schools in a safe neighborhood. Don't forget to post a note on the discussion boards to chat with women who already live there and can give you the scoop.

★ http://www.dtic.mil/perdiem/—The Per Diem Committee website allows you to look up your travel pay.

★ Naval Supply Systems Command Household Goods website at http://www.smartwebmove.navsup.navy.mil can give you estimates for the cost of your move.

★ La Quinta Inns (1-800-531-5900)—The only hotel chain that accepts two pets up to 40 pounds at all locations.

10

Marriage Hoo-ah!

CREATING A FAMILY STRATEGY
AND LIFETIME DREAMS

If successful marriages thrive with communication and planning, then unsuccessful marriages are rife with misunderstandings, misguided actions, and resentment. Contrary to most newlyweds' belief, you cannot read each other's mind. If a stranger asked my husband, for example, what he envisioned doing this coming weekend, he'd say we plan to sit on the couch and watch *SportsCenter.* If a stranger asked me, I'd respond that we plan to bathe our son, go grocery shopping, and have a romantic dinner out. Sometime between now and Friday, we will work out a plan that incorporates elements of both visions of the perfect weekend. But we have to take the time to respectfully ask each other what we want to do and then form a compromise.

If it takes this kind of communication to figure out our weekend plans, it certainly takes even more to figure out our lifetime plans. Not only does each of us have to identify and articulate our dreams and goals for the future, but we also have to compromise with each other and form a strategy to achieve the goals we each have.

Remember: Each person's goals are just as important as the other's. While it may seem easy to allow your servicemember's career in the military to dictate and drive your life's goals, it is only a recipe for resentment. And why cave in when it is possible to achieve your goals as well as his? To make our family strategy, we use a tool called the Master Plan.

First introduced in the terrific financial planning book *The Savvy Sailor*, by Ralph Nelson, the Master Plan concept starts by plotting your servicemember's career. Ask these questions:

★ What is your husband's career track? In other words, what does he want to do when he grows up?
★ Which military bases are likely to have billets for his career track?
★ When is he likely to be promoted?
★ Does he want to stay in the military for his entire career, or should he get out at some point once he's prepped himself for a civilian career? Can he get the military to provide or pay for all of his training?

Armed with this information, you can begin to create a family strategy by charting your servicemember's proposed career track. On the next page is an example from *The Savvy Sailor* for a Navy Aviation Technician (AT) named Seaman Besaw.

This career track is right on target. Notice it takes into account the military's system for relocating and deploying your servicemember (chapter 3). It alternates between sea and shore tours for the normal periods of time, and the servicemember relocates near the same regions.

From this basic career track, and using the information you learned about military finances, you can now begin to plot your servicemember's future income. Again, we will use the example from *The Savvy Sailor*, which assumes a 2.5 percent pay increase each year.

Notice this accounting does not include extra pays we already discussed, such as Family Separation Pay or Sea Pay dur-

Year	Age	Career	Rank	Location	Job
2003	20	Boot Camp/A school	E-1-2	Great Lakes, MI	Recruit
2004	21	Sea Tour	E-3	Whidbey Island, WA	Maint. Avion. Br., EAWS
2005	22	Sea Tour	E-4	Whidbey Island, WA	Maint. Avion. Br., EAWS
2006	23	Sea Tour	E-4	Whidbey Island, WA	Maint. Avion. Br., EAWS
2007	24	Sea Tour	E-5	San Diego, CA	Instr. Avion. Sch.
2008	25	Shore Tour	E-5	San Diego, CA	Instr. Avion. Sch.
2009	26	Shore Tour	E-5	San Diego, CA	Instr. Avion. Sch.
2010	27	Shore Tour	E-5	San Diego, CA	Instr. Avion. Sch.
2011	28	Adv. training	E-6	Jacksonville, FL	Student
2012	29	Sea Tour	E-6	Jacksonville, FL	Workcenter LPO
2013	30	Sea Tour	E-6	Jacksonville, FL	Workcenter LPO
2014	31	Sea Tour	E-6	Jacksonville, FL	Workcenter LPO
2015	32	Sea Tour	E-7	Jacksonville, FL	Workcenter LPO
2016	33	Shore Tour	E-7	Pensacola, FL	Recruiter
2017	34	Shore Tour	E-7	Pensacola, FL	Recruiter
2018	35	Shore Tour	E-7	Pensacola, FL	Recruiter
2019	36	Sea Tour	E-8	Jacksonville, FL	Maint. QA
2020	37	Sea Tour	E-8	Jacksonville, FL	Maint. QA
2021	38	Sea Tour	E-8	Jacksonville, FL	Maint. QA
2022	39	Sea Tour	E-8	Jacksonville, FL	Maint. QA

Adapted from Nelson, Ralph F., *The Savvy Sailor: An Eye-Opening Guide to One Sailor's Personal Financial Saga!* Rockville, MD: Master Plan, Inc., 2002

SEAMAN BESAW'S CAREER PAY

Year	Age	Rank	Base Pay	Housing	Food	Clothing	Total
2003	20	E-1-2	$13,820	0 (barracks)	$232	$261	$14,314
2004	21	E-3	$15,642	0	$310	$292	$16,243
2005	22	E-4	$18,668	0	$317	$299	$19,284
2006	23		$20,167	0	$325	$306	$20,799
2007	24		$23,629*	0	$333	$314	$24,277
2008	25	E-5	$24,220	$16,186	$3,200	$322	$43,928*
2009	26		$25,970	$16,591	$3,280	$330	$46,171
2010	27		$26,619	$17,006	$3,362	$338	$47,325
2011	28	E-6	$32,159	$11,896	$3,446	$347	$47,848
(and so on until you reach 20 years in service. . . .)							
2023	40	E-8	$55,682	$16,788	$4,522	$455	$77,446

*Note the big bump in pay in 2007. While it may seem Seaman Besaw got a pay increase for being promoted to E-5, closer inspection shows that he simply was no longer allowed to live in the barracks and opted for civilian housing. Thus, he was given BAH Without Dependents. All of it was put toward rent and utilities.

Adapted from Nelson, Ralph F., *The Savvy Sailor: An Eye-Opening Guide to One Sailor's Personal Financial Saga!* Rockville, MD: Master Plan, Inc., 2002

ing sea tours, but you can treat that as icing on the cake. For now, focus on figuring out how much money your servicemember will earn. Include pay at 20 years of service, remembering that retirement is calculated as a percentage of pay between the 20- and 30-year mark, depending on which plan you choose. Going back to our Master Plan, we can add information on pay (see chart, page 151).

Now you can begin to make your own personal, career, and family plans. Ask yourself and then discuss with your servicemember the following questions:

★ What are *your* personal and professional goals? Can your career travel with you, or do you need to be stationed in one location?

★ Do you want to try to live in one location as much as possible, or opt for some adventurous travel—or a mix of both?

★ Do you want to have kids and how do you want to raise them?

★ How can you work the military pay system to earn as much income, retirement, and education benefits as possible?

★ Can your husband hone his career track to fit your family goals?

Let's continue with the example in *The Savvy Sailor*. Seaman Besaw talked extensively with his girlfriend, Susie, and together they decided to get married at age 25, just when the seaman would be leaving his sea tour and starting a shore tour. That way, they could spend the first three years of their marriage uninterrupted by deployment. Susie, however, wanted to continue working, which was fine because San Diego (where they would be stationed) has a very high cost of living. They decided it would be better to wait until the end of his shore tour and the beginning of his advanced training to have a baby. Jacksonville, where training would take place, has a very low cost of living, so they could easily afford to have Susie quit work and stay at home with the baby if she wanted to. Following training, they would try to get a sea tour billet in Jacksonville to maintain fam-

Year	Age	Career	Rank	Location	Job	Annual Income
2003	20	Boot Camp/A school	E-1-2	Great Lakes, MI	Recruit	$14,314
2004	21	Sea Tour	E-3	Whidbey Island, WA	Maint. Avion. Br., EAWS	16,243
2005	22	Sea Tour	E-4	Whidbey Island, WA	Maint. Avion. Br., EAWS	16,243
2006	23	Sea Tour	E-4	Whidbey Island, WA	Maint. Avion. Br., EAWS	18,668
2007	24	Sea Tour	E-5	San Diego, CA	Instr. Avion. Sch.	18,668
2008	25	Shore Tour	E-5	San Diego, CA	Instr. Avion. Sch.	43,928
2009	26	Shore Tour	E-5	San Diego, CA	Instr. Avion. Sch.	43,928
2010	27	Shore Tour	E-5	San Diego, CA	Instr. Avion. Sch.	43,928
2011	28	Adv. training	E-6	Jacksonville, FL	Student	47,848
2012	29	Sea Tour	E-6	Jacksonville, FL	Workcenter LPO	49,044
2013	30	Sea Tour	E-6	Jacksonville, FL	Workcenter LPO	49,044
2014	31	Sea Tour	E-6	Jacksonville, FL	Workcenter LPO	49,044
2015	32	Sea Tour	E-7	Jacksonville, FL	Workcenter LPO	49,044
2016	33	Shore Tour	E-7	Pensacola, FL	Recruiter	60,573
2017	34	Shore Tour	E-7	Pensacola, FL	Recruiter	60,573
2018	35	Shore Tour	E-7	Pensacola, FL	Recruiter	60,573
2019	36	Sea Tour	E-8	Jacksonville, FL	Maint. QA	70,483
2020	37	Sea Tour	E-8	Jacksonville, FL	Maint. QA	70,483
2021	38	Sea Tour	E-8	Jacksonville, FL	Maint. QA	70,483
2022	39	Sea Tour	E-8	Jacksonville, FL	Maint. QA	77,446

Adapted from Nelson, Ralph F., *The Savvy Sailor: An Eye-Opening Guide to One Sailor's Personal Financial Saga!* Rockville, MD: Master Plan, Inc., 2002

ily stability with the new baby. They could also have a second child while in Jacksonville. By the end of his sea tour, their first child would be ready to start school, so the Besaws could opt to move close to home by taking a recruiting job in Pensacola. Before they relocate, however, they could afford to buy a home in Jacksonville on Seaman Besaw's salary alone. Then Seaman Besaw could opt for another sea tour billet in Jacksonville and subsequently retire at 20 years if he wished.

Using this strategy, we can add the relevant information to the Besaws' Master Plan (see chart, page 153).

The Savvy Sailor is highly recommended to help you develop a more detailed financial plan for your family (see the end of this chapter for how to obtain a copy), but even using this basic start you can begin to make out your family strategy. *The Savvy Sailor* also includes sample Master Plans for you to fill out. Once you get started, you and your servicemember will find it exciting! What an opportunity to build your marriage by sharing dreams and goals together.

A BIG "IF"

Having encouraged you to make a family strategy, I must now give you a very big caveat: *You are not guaranteed to get the billets and duty stations you want.* You and your servicemember can make the best of plans, but the military's needs change and the billets you want may not even be open for the taking.

Don't freak out. This is where communication is all the more critical to manage each other's expectations about which dreams are actually achievable or desirable. By getting into an almost daily habit of discussing dreams and the challenges to those dreams, you and your servicemember can subtly adjust each other's perceptions about what may be the right path. Then, when something doesn't go right, it's not such a shock and you've already discussed alternatives.

Year	Age	Career	Rank	Location	Job	Annual Income	Family	Susie's Career	Housing
2003	20	Boot Camp/A school	E-1-2	Great Lakes, MI	Recruit	$14,314		College	Barracks
2004	21	Sea Tour	E-3	Whidbey Island, WA	Maint. Avion. Br., EAWS	16,243		College	Barracks
2005	22	Sea Tour	E-4	Whidbey Island, WA	Maint. Avion. Br., EAWS	16,243		College	Barracks
2006	23	Sea Tour	E-4	Whidbey Island, WA	Maint. Avion. Br., EAWS	18,668		Job	Barracks
2007	24	Sea Tour	E-5	San Diego, CA	Instr. Avion. Sch.	18,668		Job	Barracks
2008	25	Shore Tour	E-5	San Diego, CA	Instr. Avion. Sch.	43,928	Marry/Baby	Job	Rent Apt.
2009	26	Shore Tour	E-5	San Diego, CA	Instr. Avion. Sch.	43,928		Homemaker	Rent Apt.
2010	27	Shore Tour	E-5	San Diego, CA	Instr. Avion. Sch.	43,928		Homemaker	Rent Apt.
2011	28	Adv. training	E-6	Jacksonville, FL	Student	47,848		Homemaker	Rent → Buy Home
2012	29	Sea Tour	E-6	Jacksonville, FL	Workcenter LPO	49,044	Baby	Homemaker	Rent → Buy Home
2013	30	Sea Tour	E-6	Jacksonville, FL	Workcenter LPO	49,044		Homemaker	Rent → Buy Home
2014	31	Sea Tour	E-6	Jacksonville, FL	Workcenter LPO	49,044		Homemaker	Rent → Buy Home
2015	32	Sea Tour	E-7	Jacksonville, FL	Workcenter LPO	49,044		Homemaker	Rent → Buy Home
2016	33	Shore Tour	E-7	Pensacola, FL	Recruiter	60,573		Continuing Ed.	Rent (Rent Out Home)
2017	34	Shore Tour	E-7	Pensacola, FL	Recruiter	60,573		Continuing Ed.	Rent (Rent Out Home)
2018	35	Shore Tour	E-7	Pensacola, FL	Recruiter	60,573		Continuing Ed.	Rent (Rent Out Home)
2019	36	Sea Tour	E-8	Jacksonville, FL	Maint. QA	70,483		Job	Home
2020	37	Sea Tour	E-8	Jacksonville, FL	Maint. QA	70,483		Job	Home
2021	38	Sea Tour	E-8	Jacksonville, FL	Maint. QA	70,483		Job	Home
2022	39	Sea Tour	E-8	Jacksonville, FL	Maint. QA	77,446		Job	Home

Adapted from Nelson, Ralph F., *The Savvy Sailor: An Eye-Opening Guide to One Sailor's Personal Financial Saga!* Rockville, MD: Master Plan, Inc., 2002

What happens if you desire a certain duty station and it doesn't come up as an option for your servicemember's next billet? The worst-case scenario is that neither you nor your servicemember did your research on that duty station to find out whether the billet was open—so the billet list came as a shock—nor did you discuss alternatives that are acceptable to both of you.

The best-case scenario is that you and your servicemember did do research on that duty station and discovered that there aren't many billets available there. There's a chance a billet might come up, but it's not very likely. With that in mind, you discuss which billets *are* likely to come up and the pros and cons of each. Part of that discussion is what your family priorities are right now. Do you want to travel to exotic places or stay close to home in a low-cost, family-friendly community? By agreeing in advance and prioritizing your preferences for duty stations, and also prioritizing your goals for the next duty station in general, you won't be surprised when the billet list arrives. You will already know which billets are preferable, even if you didn't expect to see some duty stations on the billet list.

The importance of getting into the habit of discussing your dreams and challenges also extends to your goals and aspirations. If you are a die-hard career woman and suddenly decide to stay at home with the kids, you will shock the heck out of your servicemember and probably your family finances, as well. If over time, however, you share with him your dissatisfaction with your job, concern about leaving the kids in day care, and ideas for penny-pinching if you were to stay at home, your servicemember will be on the same mental track with you and the decision won't be so traumatic.

On a final note, don't get angry with your servicemember if your family strategy has to take a detour because the billets you want aren't available. He can't control these things. He can only do his best to research what is available, discuss the options with you, negotiate with his stubborn detailer, and hope for the best. It's always tempting to take out your frustration on your servicemember, but you would be doing him an injustice for all his hard work.

CALLING ALL MILITARY MEN: BETTER WAYS TO COMMUNICATE WITH YOUR WIFE

(Ladies, this section is for your servicemember to read.)

If you have read the above section on creating a family strategy, you may be freaking out right now. *How can this crazy woman suggest to my wife that we have any control over billets?* you're thinking. *The less my wife knows about available billets, the less she has to worry about.*

This approach is very typical of men who truly just want to make their wives happy. Unfortunately, men and women deal with stress differently. Military men often encourage their wives to "go with the flow" and *expect* to be sent to Timbuktu. Yet no comment will piss off your wife more because she wants to *feel* control over her destiny. The family strategy approach suggested herein will allow her to *feel* in control of the situation, even if you aren't actually in control and don't get the billets you want. It's the communication and compromise that are important. How does this work?

First, understand that by insisting your wife accept lack of control over the situation, you are indirectly telling her that her dreams don't matter to you or the military. By allowing billets to dictate your family's direction, you are saying your job has priority over her dreams.

By contrast, your wife wants to know you are listening to her dreams and priorities because they count for something in your marriage. And when you listen to her dreams, you are informing yourself about what kind of billets are acceptable to her. Then you can come home and say, "You know how you've always wanted to go to Hawaii? Well, I'm not sure the rumor is true, but I heard today that there may be a position opening

Marriage Hoo-ah!

155

around the time I'm supposed to get my next orders. Let me find out more information so I can see how likely this would be, but I wanted to let you know." You will get the best sex of your life.

What happens if that Hawaii billet isn't available? Keep her posted on what information you learn so you can manage her expectations. Don't try to shelter her by saying nothing if you hear bad news—share it with her. What's most important about this process is that you are letting her know that you are doing your best to make her dreams come true. If you've done what you can and the billet doesn't come through, she will know how much you love her and appreciate the effort. In the meantime, you should also be discussing her priorities on billets you know will be open. When those billets show up on the list of options, your wife will be prepared to accept them and confident that you have made the right decision.

Notice how none of this has to do with actually controlling the billet situation. Instead, this is all about *perceived* control over the situation because you both have a genuine grasp of what your priorities are as a family. By listening and showing appreciation for your wife's dreams, you are giving her a sense of control. And that makes her happy!

HANDLING DEPLOYMENT
SEPARATION TOGETHER

After the stress of feeling out of control of your life and marriage, deployment and separation are the second hardest things on military marriages. As noted before, long-term absence typically does not make the heart grow fonder—it makes it more resentful. So you want to limit the chance and length of deployments to the extent you can, using your family strategy. There are exceptions to this rule, however, and they can apply to the deployments that will inevitably occur.

Experienced military wives handle deployments more suc-

SERVICEMEMBERS:
WHAT TO SAY TO YOUR WIFE

Never say . . .	Instead, say this . . .
Go with the flow.	These are the duty stations that are likely to be available, given my career track. Which ones are you interested in?
We'll never be able to get a post at . . .	To get a post at . . . , it will mean I have to do X, Y, and Z, and we will probably have to live at A. That seems like quite a challenge for our family. Are you sure you want to do that?
I don't know what billets will be available. No one ever does! I don't care what your friends say.	It's hard to say at this point, but given my career track, I'm likely to get billets at A, B, and C. Which of those interest you? —or— Let's go through the possible scenarios.
I refuse to live there!	I really do not want to take that billet. The job is really bad and would require me to do X, Y, and Z. I could see my unhappiness would really make the family miserable. Isn't there another billet you might find acceptable?
I know you heard there might be a position open at X, but there's no way we'll get it.	Interesting news! However, I have heard that that position requires someone with more qualifications than I have. Why don't I do some more research and see what I can find out.

Marriage Hoo-ah!

cessfully for two reasons. First, they and their servicemembers have created avenues for continuing communication and romance across the distance. The Internet makes it even easier. Regular communication allows the servicemember to stay involved in the family's daily life and remain a principal parent and decision maker. By keeping the servicemember informed about the family's daily activities, you don't have to write a book to explain and ask advice on the inevitable crises that will pop up during his absence. He will already be up-to-date on what's brewing and can quickly respond with his thoughts.

It's important that this regular sharing of information not be a one-way stream of complaints from you. Be assured that your servicemember misses you heartily, and he is worried about leaving you on your own no matter how competent you are. Most of all, he feels guilty. To top it off, he is probably working like a dog and clocking 18-hour days doing dangerous tasks. When you send him nothing but complaints, you worsen his negative feelings and may even distract him from his job. Not only does this ultimately hurt your marriage, it may make him dangerous to himself and his colleagues. There is absolutely nothing your servicemember can do to make you feel better about deployment and handling life on your own. He cannot leave his station, and he cannot come to your rescue. So please think before you write.

Successful military families are also talented digital photographers and web masters. To share their daily lives together, they regularly take pictures and videos to exchange by e-mail or place on a family website. It is just as important for the servicemember to take pictures as it is for the kids. How else can you understand what his job entails or get to know his colleagues and friends? (Note: Obviously, any servicemember in special operations is exempt from this because his job is classified. So don't get mad at him!)

With this daily information-sharing, leaving for deployment and returning home become much easier transitions. Your servicemember will already be aware of and support any new rules you have imposed on your children, and he will feel less guilty about having left his family. He won't feel the need to spoil the kids with ice cream every night or let them bend every rule. You and the kids, in turn, will not view him as a total stranger when he returns, nor resent him when he tries to reassert his authority as a parent and reassume his role as a spouse.

Along with the sharing of daily family news, successful military couples keep up the intensity of their romance through regular communication. While X-rated e-mails are inappropriate because all e-mail into the unit may be read for security purposes, you can develop a more subtle approach using coded words that only he knows. Also, don't send pornographic pictures of yourself, or you may find them plastered all over the Internet. Instead, send him regular care packages with his favorite foods, phone cards, and less risqué pictures of you and the kids.

On the other side of the relationship, he should call you whenever possible, even if it is only for a few minutes. If he can talk for only a short time, assure him how grateful you are just to hear his voice. He will find a way to call you back, even if it means waiting in the phone line for hours! Along the same lines, be sure to let him know how much you enjoy hearing about his day and receiving pictures. He'll appreciate your interest in his life and feel that you understand the stress he is under.

If regular communication is the primary force behind suc-

★★★ **DID YOU KNOW?** ★★★

Experienced military wives often actually look forward to deployment. They see it as an opportunity to do the things they wouldn't otherwise have time to do, such as continuing their education, taking a karate or ballet class, or just spending more time with friends and family members.

Marriage Hoo-ah!

cessful military marriages, a sense of independence and self-esteem on your part is the other element.

Struggling wives spend too much time wallowing in their own depression. They honestly believe that the sole source of their happiness is their servicemember—as if they'd never been happy in their entire lives before they met him! They spend a lot of time moping on the couch.

If you are one of these wives, my advice is to get up and get busy. Surely there are tons of things you've always wanted to do but never had the opportunity—so go do them! While you're at it, go meet friends for dinner. And volunteer to help people less fortunate than you are. They will be your reminder of how lucky you are to be you.

One of the best ways to keep busy is to get involved with your command family support unit to prepare an elaborate homecoming party. This amazing event is often on the minds of families and servicemembers everywhere, and your servicemember and his colleagues will gossip like hens about what the families have planned. The possibilities are endless and get more elaborate every year. My personal favorite is the 400-plus-foot flower leis that Navy families often string around the ship when it arrives in port. This is your chance to show off your creativity and let your servicemember know how much you're looking forward to his return.

Finally, while your servicemember is deployed, you will need the resources to take care of yourself and your family. Plan ahead before deployment to make sure these resources are available. For example, mothers of young children should plan for a baby-sitter once per week so you can get out of the house and away from the kids. Whether you pay for a baby-sitter or have your mom baby-sit, make the arrangements in advance so you don't get stuck. Similarly, working moms need to find logistical support services and the money to pay for them. Whether it's day care, emergency baby-sitters, laundry services, or grocery delivery, you will need help in replacing the extra hand your servicemember provided when he was home. By planning ahead, you can prevent and diffuse the inevitable crises that will pop up during deployments.

EXTRA PARENTING SKILLS
FOR MILITARY COUPLES

Military parents need extra skills to help their kids cope with military life. Military kids move frequently and have to make friends quickly and start at new schools. My own mother, a Navy brat, moved 14 times in 16 years.

Military kids also face the loneliness of separation from their parent during deployments and, worse, may worry about their parent's safety. Indeed, too much CNN for kids is not a good thing!

I've talked about the importance of getting your family settled into a new community as quickly after relocation as possible. Start with setting up your kids' room to look as much like their old room as possible. Choose decorations, including wall art, that can travel with you.

Before you relocate, identify fun activities in your new hometown and sign your kids up. With any luck, by the second week of moving in your kids will already be distracted from the stress of moving and focused on having fun with new friends. If you can manage it, invite your new neighbors over for a barbeque so your kids can meet other kids on the block.

Above all, encourage your kids to be as social as possible. This is tougher for shy kids, but an important skill to succeed. You can help them by practicing how to introduce themselves to friends, engage in conversation, and share toys.

Deployments are more difficult because you face emotional issues similar to those in divorce. Your kids may feel like the parent is leaving them because of something they did, so be straightforward with your children that deployment is just part of Daddy's or Mommy's job and that he or she is coming back as soon as the job is done. Immediately after breaking the news of deployment, begin discussing ways to keep in touch in order to reassure your kids that the parent is still a part of the family.

For example, buy an inexpensive camera for your kids to take pictures with and send to the deployed parent. They can even take the camera to school and snap photos of friends. Older kids can get started on developing a family website on which to place pictures and videos. Another good idea is to get the kids involved in planning homecoming activities as soon as the servicemember leaves. Maybe homecoming is a good time to plan a family vacation at Disneyland? If so, the servicemember can put in for leave now.

Finally, let the kids know that just because Daddy is gone doesn't mean he's not still in charge as a parent. Similarly, if a stepparent is being left in charge of the kids, the servicemember must insist that her word goes while he's gone. The kids should understand that the parents are keeping in touch and will continue to administer discipline as a team. By keeping Daddy involved, you will feel like you still have a backup parent and the kids will respect his authority when he comes home. Daddy will also feel relieved that he is still valued as a parent.

When Daddy is involved in war or combat, the stress of deployment goes to a higher level. Again, you need to be straight-

★★★ DID YOU KNOW? ★★★

When discussing issues of discipline with your kids, be sure to mention that your servicemember was included in the decision making. For example, you can tell your little girl that Mommy and Daddy agreed that she is too young right now to get her ears pierced, but that Daddy said he would take her to get it done when he got back from deployment. This prevents you from being the "bad guy" all the time.

forward with kids that Daddy is at war, but reassure them how strong and courageous he is and that he and his troops will prevail. It helps to discuss combat in terms of "fighting the bad guys" because it makes kids proud of what their parent is doing and justifies the sacrifice of separation. Young children are also reassured by the idea that a guardian angel is watching over Daddy and "the good guys."

If you absolutely need to watch CNN, do it on your own time and limit your kids' exposure. They don't need their worries about Daddy increased and imprinted on their little brains. Also, watch television with your kids and make sure they know the difference between violence on TV and real violence. It sometimes helps if Daddy explains what it is really like on the battlefield (deleting any explicit references to gory details, of course) compared to what is shown on TV.

During deployments, it's important to keep teachers and other adults notified so that they can warn you of any trouble and work with you to counsel your kids on dealing with the stress. Schools located near military bases frequently have specialized counselors on hand for this exact reason—so don't be afraid to use their knowledge if you need help. Finally, remember that your kids need a break from you, too. Schedule time for them with friends or favorite baby-sitters so they can do fun things and not worry about their family.

The Least You Need to Know

★ A solid military marriage requires planning your life together and constantly communicating your dreams and ways to overcome obstacles.

★ While you cannot guarantee you'll get the billets you want, you can limit the chance of getting a particularly nasty billet by researching and planning ahead.

★ Deployment is stressful on marriage, but you can get through by maintaining regular communication and keeping busy with friends and fun activities. Experienced wives actually look forward to deployments!

★ Military parents need to help their kids learn social skills and get settled into new communities quickly. They must also ease the stress of deployments on kids through honest communication, regular contact, and maintaining two-parent discipline. Combat deployments require extra sensitivity to kids' worries about the safety of their parent.

Resources

★ *The Savvy Sailor* (http://www.savvy.onweb.com)—This terrific book explains the details of military financial planning while telling a romantic story of a couple who fall in love and get married. Even though it's written for sailors, all servicemembers can benefit.

11

The Adventures of
Military Life

Military life can be very exciting, and not just because you can get a military discount at most stores (be sure to ask!). There are tips and tricks for making things fun and easy, and this chapter reviews just a few of them:

1. Furnishing a military household with worldwide treasures
2. How to vacation at almost no cost
3. Children's activities and hobbies (for kids ages 2 to 92)

FURNISHING A MILITARY HOUSEHOLD

Whether you're a bride-to-be or a seasoned military wife, it is always a good idea to consider the military lifestyle when buying furniture or household items. Similarly, as you purchase souvenirs from your travels, you want to make sure you're investing in something that will stand the test of time and home decor. After all, these can be high-priced items that will hopefully last a lifetime or longer. There are two things to consider when stocking up your household inventory: frequent moving and the need for storage.

The typical military family moves every three years. That means having burly guys (including your husband) pack up your good china and collectibles. So consider the following tips:

★ When entering military life, it's probably not a good idea to start collecting antique teacups or glass figurines.

★ Select durable china patterns such as Wedgwood with colors that are baked in instead of painted on. Patterns with gold rims may look durable, but it is really gold paint that chips off in the dishwasher.

★ Choose thick crystal or glassware instead of the delicate, thin kind.

★ Let professional movers pack your china and breakables, but tell them how delicate they are. They'll do a better job than you will.

Military families also tend to live in base housing or rentals—and that means a lot of white walls, kitchens, and bathrooms. Despite your best decorating intentions, you are not likely to paint, so you're better off strategizing with a solid decorating theme that will look good whether you're stationed in Japan or California or Washington, DC.

★ When buying your first pieces of furniture, select a general color scheme for the entire house. Every time you buy a new piece, make sure it fits into that scheme—even if it is for a different room. In a few years, all of your furniture may end up in the same room together, so it has to coordinate.

★ Do not select color schemes with neutral colors like white, beige, or black. Your walls in base housing or rental homes will always be white or beige, so you'll need to brighten things up with color.

★ Buy wooden picture frames and shelves that can be painted. It's a great way to spiff up the inevitable white walls of your base housing or rental.

★ Recognize that "California Casual"–style furniture does not look good everywhere. When selecting the cloth for your furniture, choose patterns that will fit in wherever you go. Then use inexpensive tablecloths, curtains, and decorative pillows to make your look more casual or formal.

★ Good-quality used wood, antique, or foreign-made furniture are great collectibles, they're inexpensive, and they capture the memories of where you once lived. In Washington, DC, for example, you can get a beautiful dark-wood clothes drawer (circa 1900) at local antique fairs for around $70. Japanese "stair" chests are another great investment.

★ When you've finally convinced your husband that the Budweiser Girls are not considered art, contemplate buying a mirror instead of a large poster or painting. They're less expensive than good art, and they brighten a room and go with all decor.

Finally, the biggest challenge for military families is switching from single-family homes in low-cost areas to apartments or town homes in high-cost areas. How do you fit an entire house full of furniture into an apartment without giving half of it away? Below are some tips to address all these problems:

★ Invest in a good sofa bed. They're more expensive than regular sofas, but you can put them in the living room *or* in a guest room.

★ Use laminated bookshelves that must be assembled but can be taken apart for easy storage. Buy one neutral color (such as black or white) so that they can be mixed and matched in any room. They can be used for books, children's rooms, clothes

MORE IDEAS FROM LINDSEY OF
SHEPPARD AFB, TEXAS

Use liquid fabric starch to adhere fabric to walls. Small pieces of cutout fabric can be used as "stencils," and larger pieces of fabric (including flat bedsheets) work as "wallpaper."

Simply immerse your desired fabric, already cut to shape, in a bucket of liquid fabric starch (available at most commissaries for less than $2 a bottle). Wring out any excess. Using a sponge dampened with water, smooth the fabric onto the wall, pressing out any air bubbles. Wipe any drips with a damp sponge or cloth. Allow the fabric to dry. When it is time to move, fill a spritzer bottle with water and gently moisten the fabric on the walls. The fabric will easily peel away, leaving the walls clean and white again!

While in Europe, I made simple curtains for my child's bedroom. Using cut patches of the extra fabric, I created a stencil effect on the walls. When it was time to PCS, I packed the curtains and the stencil patches into a bag and took them to the thrift shop, along with the "how-to" directions. They sold right away, and now another child's room has been decorated with very little effort!

storage in closets, and bathrooms, or dismantled and packed away in minimal space.

★ For storing china, consider buying corner cabinets instead of traditional rectangular monstrosities that take up an entire wall. Triangular in shape, corner cabinets hold a lot more than you think and can fit in almost any room. They're harder to find, but you can usually buy them in any style at your favorite furniture store.

★ When choosing bedside tables or end tables, select ones with drawers for extra storage space.

★ Get a library card. Buying books costs more money than you think, and their accumulated weight takes up too much of your allocated shipping weight. They also require a lot of storage.

★ Avoid buying tchotchkes, trinkets, or bric-a-brac—especially delicate items—at any cost. If you want to collect memories, get your family interested in photography. Inexpensive jewelry is another option that collects less dust and requires less space.

★ Every three months, make your entire family review their clothes and belongings and give away any item that has not been used in the last year. Not only will this improve storage and packing time, it will force every family member to think twice before buying something.

If you do have to give away furniture and sundries, make an effort to give them to another military family. We all reap the benefits in the end.

HOW TO VACATION AT ALMOST NO COST

Did you know you can fly to Europe for a family vacation at the military's expense? Space Available or "Space A" flights are one of the great benefits of military life. Essentially, the military has regular transport planes of all types flying around the world. Not only do they move equipment, they transport relocating families and officials on business. Often, there is plenty of extra space available on overseas flights to take on passengers, so the military allows servicemembers and their dependents to fly "Space Available." The military is also testing the possibility of allowing family members to fly Space A within CONUS.

The trick is that, while the flights run on a regular schedule, there is no guarantee a seat will be available for you. You may have to wait for the next flight or the flight after that before boarding a jet to Italy. Also, the flights can be downright bare, so pro travelers suggest bringing plenty of food and blankets.

The pros say the downsides are still worth the ability to travel globally. Desiring romantic time together before a six-month deployment, my girlfriend Belle and her Marine husband spent two weeks in Italy over Easter. When their return flight wasn't immediately available in Italy, they used the excuse to spend a couple days in Germany and fly home from there. To save money, the couple stayed at base lodging and packed lunches from the commissaries. It was the experience of a lifetime—at a grand total cost of $500 for the whole trip!

Base lodging is another great deal. Nearly all military bases worldwide offer the ability to stay at a base "lodge" or hotel or the Bachelor Enlisted/Officer's Quarters (**BEQ** or **BOQ**). Some of these are so popular they get booked a year in advance. Our favorite places include the BOQ and Navy Lodge at NAS North Island, on the white beaches of San Diego, and the Navy Lodge at NAS Key West, where you can rent a motorboat for a few dollars per day. More famous destinations are the Hale Koa military hotel on Waikiki Beach in Hawaii and the Shades of Green resort for military families at Disneyworld in Orlando, Florida.

While there are a number of lodging and Transportation Command websites (https://amcpublic.scott.af.mil/spacea/spacea.htm) with Space A schedules and regulations, I recommend investing in copies of *Military Space-A Air* and *Temporary Military Lodging Around the World,* published by Military Living Publications. These and other terrific guides, such as *Military RV, Camping & Outdoor Recreation Around the World,* can be found at your base Exchange or online at http://www.military living.com.

CHILDREN'S ACTIVITIES
(FOR KIDS FROM 2 TO 92)

Because so many military families have young children, the Morale, Welfare, and Recreation (MWR) offices and Marine Corps Community Services (MCCS) offer tons of activities for families with children.

One of my regular stops is the Information, Tickets & Tours (ITT) office for free or significantly discounted tickets to rock concerts, theaters, movies, kids' events, and major theme parks, including Disneyland and Busch Gardens. ITT also frequently puts together travel packages for groups of families to visit more distant locations, particularly theme parks. It's worth a quick stop to receive a flyer with all available discounts listed.

MWR and MCCS also offer summer day camps and after-school activities ranging from sports to arts and crafts. Adults can get in on the fun at the numerous woodworking shops, pottery classes, and other activities offered by MWR and MCCS. My favorite class so far has been Kahuna Bob's Surfing Lessons at Camp Pendleton, California.

For those who want to get outside, MWR and MCCS rent outdoor and party equipment for pennies. This equipment is typically tailored to your local area, so you will find horse trailers and stables in rural areas and beach tents and chairs near the coastlines. Folding chairs and tables and other equipment are also available for parties.

Finally, every military base offers plenty of recreation and athletic facilities. The Air Force is famous for its golf courses and the Navy for its beaches. Most bases also have several pool facilities, including many at the center of base housing complexes, and the best gymnasiums, with top-of-the-line equipment and the latest aerobics classes. Most bases operate team sports leagues and competitions for both adults and children, so visit your nearest gym for brochures on upcoming events and activities.

The Least You Need to Know

★ When buying household furniture, be aware that items have to fit with the decor of your entire household in any location around the world.

★ Collecting furniture and photos from the places where you live is a great way to save memories while minimizing clutter.

★ The freebies you get in the military mean you can plan a virtually cost-free vacation.

★ MWR and MCCS are your source for unique and fun activities for you and the kids. Check that office and the base newspaper regularly for the latest events and offers.

Resources

★ Space A Flights (https://amcpublic.scott.af.mil/spacea/spacea.htm)—Find free flights anywhere in the world.

★ Military Living Publications (http://www.militaryliving.com)—Terrific books on cheap travel deals through the military.

★ The Navy Lodge (http://www.navy-lodge.com).

★ http://www.armymwr.com, http://www.mwr.navy.mil, http://www.afsv.af.mil, and http://www.usmc-mccs.org—The national websites for MWR and MCCS, but be sure to check your base website for local MWR or MCCS sites promoting activities and resources in your area.

★ Marine Corps Community Services (http://www.usmc-mccs.org/).

★ Air Force Crossroads (http://www.afcrossroads.com/activities/index.cfm)—This section has tons of travel and recreation activities.

★ Navy LifeLines (http://www.lifelines2000.org)—The website for Navy family services and activities.

★ Check your base website for local MWR or MCCS activities.

12

What Happens When the Worst Happens— and What to Do

No one expects the worst to happen, so we tend not to plan in advance. Fortunately, the military does, and there are resources in place to support you and your family in times of need.

WHEN A SERVICEMEMBER DIES

When an active duty servicemember dies, a command representative and the Decedent Affairs Officer (in the Army, the Notification Officer) come to inform the family. The Decedent Affairs Officer helps make funeral arrangements and "invitational travel orders" for immediate family members to attend the funeral.

Then the Casualty Assistance Calls Officers (CACOs)—in the Army, the Casualty Assistance Officers—help survivors apply for the benefits entitled to them. Sometimes the CACO comes with a $6,000 check in hand for the death gratuity, the purpose of which is primarily to cover funeral expenses. The surviving dependents are also entitled to Dependents Indemnity Compensation from the Veterans Administration and Service-members' Group Life Insurance (SGLI—yes, that $16.95 per month may come in handy one day). Finally, a surviving spouse is entitled to receive Survivor Benefit Compensation as part of the servicemember's retired pay, if the servicemember died while still on active duty but was otherwise eligible to retire.

WHEN YOU MUST LIVE NEAR AN AILING FAMILY MEMBER

If you must temporarily live near your immediate family, such as your parents or children living with an ex-spouse, servicemembers can be considered for a Humanitarian Transfer to a duty station nearby. They may have to delay their career progress, they may not enjoy their position, and they may not even be stationed on a base in their service. The main point, however, is not to deny a servicemember his or her right to help a family member in extreme need.

IF YOU MUST SEPARATE FROM AN ABUSIVE SPOUSE

The 1995 DoD Authorization Act requires the Armed Forces to provide monthly payments to spouses and eligible children of active duty servicemembers who are separated from the military due to family abuse. This compensation may be awarded for a period of one to three years. The purpose is to prevent financial hardship on spouses who report abuse and whose servicemembers are incarcerated as a result. Contact the Family Advocacy representative in your base Family Support Center for more information.

WHEN YOUR SERVICEMEMBER'S PAY GETS SCREWED UP AND YOU HAVE NO MONEY FOR GROCERIES OR BILLS

Pay problems happen all the time because of administrative errors as well as mismanagement due to the complicated nature of our benefits. For example, when a servicemember goes on an extended deployment, his pay is docked for BAS since he will now be eating with his unit. That's big bucks to a wife who had counted on that money to make ends meet. The Navy–Marine Corps Relief Society, Army Emergency Relief, Air Force Aid Society, and American Red Cross were set up to help families with financial planning and provide interest-free loans and grants for temporary financial problems.

WHEN YOU HAVE EMERGENCY EXPENSES

Whether the car suddenly breaks down or you need money to visit your dying parent, the Navy–Marine Corps Relief Society, Army Emergency Relief, Air Force Aid Society, and American Red Cross can provide interest-free loans and grants for qualifying emergencies.

WHEN YOU DESPERATELY NEED TO TRACK DOWN A DEPLOYED SERVICEMEMBER

The American Red Cross can send emergency messages to deployed servicemembers—but only if they are genuine emergencies. It is absolutely critical that you know your servicemember's Social Security number, rank, unit, and location (such as a base, camp, or ship). Don't be a nitwit by not knowing these obviously important details! Call your base operator for the number to the American Red Cross on base. Red Cross offices located off base may not be aware of this service provided to military family members.

WHEN BOTH PARENTS OR A SINGLE PARENT IS IN THE MILITARY AND FORCED TO DEPLOY

The military tries to work with dual-servicemember families to ensure the kids are cared for. Otherwise, it risks losing both servicemembers because of the difficulty of parenting. Unfortunately, if both parents or a single servicemember is called to deploy, the parent has no choice but to deploy. There are extremely rare exceptions, but don't count on being one. By being excused from deployment, the servicemember's duties are an extra burden on the shoulders of his or her colleagues.

Additionally, the military does not provide for the cost of child care during deployments. Your only choice is to anticipate deployments and plan ahead with family and friends to care for your child. Dual-servicemember parents and single-servicemember parents are required to submit forms known as a Family Care Plan. This plan not only shows that you have thought through who will take care of your children but that you have obtained the caregiver's consent and have filled out all of the necessary legal and financial documents that will put the plan into effect, should you deploy. Failure to maintain a current Family Care Plan on file with your unit is grounds for separation from the service.

13

Preventing Trouble in Paradise

Having seen so many women succeed or struggle with military life, I've found that there are generally eight predictors of success:

1. *Embracing the benefits and keeping a positive outlook*—Mental attitude and the ability to adapt to change is the major predictor of success or struggle with military life. If you can look for opportunity in every change of circumstance, you will have the experience of a lifetime and amazing stories to tell your friends back home. For example, if you are assigned to a billet in London, England, would you rather remember the experience as dining with the Queen or being forced to live thousands of miles away from your home country and not meeting any new friends? It's the same location, but the experience is up to you. Personally, I'd rather dine with the Queen.

2. *Learning about military life and what to expect*—Some women express their resentment at the perceived lack of control over their lives by refusing to learn about military life. Yet if your servicemember held a civilian job, would you refuse to let him talk about it at home or meet his colleagues? Not only is

this attitude harmful to your marriage, it hampers your ability to get the information needed to control your family's destiny. If you resent military life, express it in a less self-destructive way.

3. *Being able to "cut the cord"*—Some women have always dreamed of traveling the world; other women are miserable at the prospect of moving away from their parents. If you are of the latter, know that you can stay close to home if you develop a solid family strategy with your servicemember that plots out his career and identifies billets located near home. Be aware, however, that circumstances may change and send your family off to Timbuktu—literally. If you simply cannot fathom the idea of being away from your hometown for two years, military life may not be for you.

4. *Asking for help when appropriate*—Everyone needs help at some point in their lives. You are not alone. However, the worst thing you can do is refuse to get help while your crisis gets worse and worse. This is particularly true with regard to financial problems, depression, and domestic abuse. The military community is standing by with a cadre of financial counselors and free loans, psychiatrists and marital counselors, and the entire Family Advocacy Program to handle these issues, respectively. Similarly, there are approximately 700,000 active duty military wives—not to mention all the veteran wives—who know what you're going through and can lend a hand. Get help before your problem turns into a major crisis.

5. *Being your own woman*—Most marriages start out with the couple being exceptionally close. Yet with military life, deployment is a question of when—not whether—he will go. It takes a sense of independence and self-esteem to be able to handle life on your own again, and then reunite with your servicemember for an even more romantic and fulfilling marriage. The most experienced military wives I know actually look forward to deployment in some ways. They use the extra time and indepen-

dence to take classes, spend time with friends, and do fun things they otherwise wouldn't have time to do. Less successful military wives sit on the couch and mope. Which gal do you want to be?

6. *Never letting the system get the best of you*—Nothing is more irritating than women who play dumb and expect others to take care of things for them. Not only is this behavior obnoxious and self-demeaning, these women are leaving their fate in the hands of people who really don't care. And then they wonder why their lives are so bad!

7. *Turning off CNN and listening to your command about information on your servicemember's safety*—Many newbie wives thrive on CNN because they think it will be the quickest way to get information about their deployed servicemember. They don't realize that the American news media is designed to sell one thing: drama. From this drama inevitably come speculation and rumors about what actually happened and how bad the situation really is. Don't fall into this trap! Turn off the television! It may be delayed, but your command admin or family support leader has more (and more detailed) information regarding your servicemember's *exact* status.

8. *Setting the standard of perfection*—Some women think they're cool by driving over the speed limit on base, dressing like tramps, and getting drunk at command functions. But this is not high school. You are socializing with your husband's bosses and colleagues, and you need to behave as such. You may be harming your servicemember's career prospects—and therefore your income potential!—by acting wildly. So grow up already!

I am convinced that all women of every personality type are capable of succeeding in military life. Sure, we all sometimes stray down the path of frustration and resentment. Who doesn't?

Civilian life has its downsides, too. But in the end we can have the adventure of a lifetime. The question is: What kind of adventure will you have?

I look forward to hearing your cocktail party stories.

14

Really Stupid Acronyms and Jargon

O kay, I admit that acronyms and jargon can be useful—and all wives and women in uniform must get to know them. But that doesn't mean the whole thing hasn't gotten out of control. Below is a translation of the lingo that will serve you well.

AAFES—*Army and Air Force Exchange Service* (pronounced "a-fees"). Operates the Exchanges or department stores on Army and Air Force Bases. (See also "PX.")

ACS—*Army Community Services.* See "FSC."

AFB—*Air Force Base.* Example: "Lackland AFB in San Antonio, Texas."

AFRTS—*Armed Forces Radio and Television Services.* Military TV and radio.

AFSA—*Air Force Services Agency.* See "MWR."

AFTB—*Army Family Team Building.* An Army program to empower and encourage family members to be self-sufficient and mission-ready.

Allotment—An amount of money set aside from your monthly paycheck and paid directly to a specified individual. Many servicemembers use an allotment to pay rent or creditors.

ANCOC—*Advanced Noncommissioned Officer Course.*

BAH—*Basic Allowance for Housing.* A key component of your pay

181

that is supposed to cover the local cost of housing for either a single servicemember or a family.

BAS—*Basic Allowance for Subsistence.* The servicemember's food allowance.

Basic Pay—The main component of military pay. Based on pay grade.

BDU—*Battle Dress Uniform.* The Navy's term for a camouflage uniform. As if there isn't enough for a newbie to learn, the Navy refuses to call this uniform what it is. Many a newbie wife (and her husband) have been embarrassed at the uniform supply store over this term.

BHA—*Basic Housing Allowance.* See "BAH."

Billet—A Navy job or position handed down by the gods known as "detailers."

BNCOC—*Basic Noncommissioned Officer Course.*

BOQ/BEQ—*Bachelor Officer's Quarters/Bachelor Enlisted Quarters.* Where single officers, single enlisted, and geographical bachelors live. If space is available, where you and your husband may stay on vacations (other than the service lodges) on military sites, or where your husband stays while on a base deployment.

BUPERS—The Navy's *Bureau of Personnel.*

BX—See "PX."

CDS—*Child Development Services.* Inexpensive day care on base.

CINC—*Commander in Chief* (pronounced "sink"), i.e., the President of the United States. The term used to refer to the highest-ranking commander in the theater of operation; for example, CINCPAC in the Pacific.

CinCHouse—*Commander in Chief of the House* (pronounced "sink house"). Jargon for the lady of the household and the ultimate authority to whom the servicemember reports. Sample use: "Soldier, I know you want to go on that spec ops mission to Outer Mongolia, but have you checked to see if that's okay with CinCHouse and the kids?"

CO—*Commanding Officer.* The head honcho of the unit.

COLA—*Cost of Living Adjustment.* An increase or decrease in pay, depending on how expensive or cheap it is to live in your area. COLA increases, for example, when you live overseas or in cities like Washington, DC. It bottoms out in places like Jacksonville, North Carolina.

Commissary—The military-run grocery store on base. You can save up to 44 percent on groceries just by shopping there!

CONUS—*Continental United States.*

CPO—*Civilian Personnel Office.* The place to get a job with the government or on base.

DeCa—*Defense Commissary Agency.* See "Commissary."

DEERS—*Defense Enrollment Eligibility Reporting Service.* The personnel department of the military that determines which benefits you're entitled to.

Deploy—To go out on a mission for a lengthy period of time.

DEROS—*Date of Estimated Return from Overseas.* The big homecoming! When the servicemember is expected to return from an overseas assignment.

Detailer—The god (or demon) responsible for job and duty station assignments. Pay homage to this person, or be assigned to the hinterlands for a three-year tour. In the Army, this is known as an assignments officer.

DFAS—*Defense Finance and Accounting Service.* The bean counters of the Department of Defense and the folks responsible for paying you accurately.

DH—*Deployed Hubby.* Mostly an Internet thing.

DITY Move—*Do-It-Yourself move.* To relocate your household goods yourself, without the help of professional movers.

DLA—*Dislocation Allowance.* The pay you receive to cover the cost of relocation.

Duty Station—The location to which a servicemember is assigned to work. Also called "post," although "post" can also refer to the base itself. Confused yet?

ETS—*Expiration Term of Service.* The date the servicemember is scheduled to get out of the military unless he or she reenlists.

Exchange—See "PX."

FFSC—*Fleet & Family Support Center.* See "FSC."

FSC—*Family Support Center* or *Family Services Center.* The base office that helps military families with everything from relocation to financial counseling.

GS—*General Schedule.* Example: GS 9. Refers to the rank of a civilian government employee, with GS 1 being the lowest peon; you won't see anything much above GS 15.

High-3—One of two types of pension plans for military retirees. The other type is REDUX.

ITT—*Information, Tickets & Tours.* A great place to get cheap tickets for rock concerts, movies, and even Disneyland!

Key Volunteer—A family support group leader (usually a wife) for a unit in the Marine Corps.

LES—*Leave and Earnings Statement.* Your monthly pay stub, which also happens to tell you how much vacation (leave) time the service-member has.

L.I.N.K.S.—*Lifestyle Insights Networking Knowledge and Skills.* This is the Marine Corps version of AFTB, where they teach the basics of getting around the green side, how to read an LES, where things are on your base, how to survive life as a military (Marine) spouse, and more.

MCB—*Marine Corps Base.* Example: "MCB Camp Pendleton."

MCCS—*Marine Corps Community Services.* See "FSC" and "MWR."

MCX—See "PX."

MRE—*Meals Ready to Eat.* The crappy freeze-dried meal that your husband will talk about when he gets back from hardship deployment. Best seasoned by Taco Bell hot sauce packets sent in care packages.

MTF—*Military Treatment Facility.* A military hospital or health care clinic.

MWR—*Morale, Welfare, and Recreation.* This office is like that of the Cruise Director on the *Love Boat:* always full of ideas on fun things to do.

NB—*Naval Base.* Example: "NB San Diego."

NCO—*Noncommissioned Officer.* Enlisted senior management.

NCOIC—*Noncommissioned Officer in Charge.*

O Club—*The Officers' Club.* Official restaurant and bar of the officers. The enlisted have their own club, although many bases are integrating both clubs into one. Officers and enlisted are not allowed to be overly social because of the need to maintain professional boundaries. So they let it all hang out when they're among their own ranks.

OCONUS—*Outside the Continental United States.* Overseas; or Hawaii, Alaska, or Puerto Rico.

OCS—*Officer Candidate School.* Where newly recruited officer "candidates" in the Army, Navy, and USMC must spend approximately 13 weeks without their families to learn the ways of the military. They will come back spouting acronyms and probably make up a few of their own.

OIC—*Officer in Charge.* The guy to call when you can't find your husband in an emergency.

OIS—*Officer Indoctrination School.* The diet version of OCS.

Ombudsman—A family support group leader (usually a wife) for a command in the Navy.

OOC—*Out of Commission.* i.e., "broken." Don't ask why they can't just say "broken."

Orders—An instruction from the military for a servicemember to leave his command and to go to a new billet (i.e., job). Your orders indicate the dates when the servicemember will separate from his old command and when he is due at his new command, as well as information on the relocation process.

OTC—*Officer Training Course.* Same as officer training school but for the Air Force.

Pay Grade—The category that determines your servicemember's level of Basic Pay. Pay grade is tied to rank. Thus, an Air Force Airman and a Navy Seaman Apprentice both have a pay grade of E-2. An Army Major and a Navy Lieutenant Commander both have a pay grade of O-4.

PCM—*Primary Care Manager.* Your main doctor, assigned by Tricare.

PCS—*Permanent Change of Station.* The term is actually used as the verb "to relocate." Example: "My family is PCSing to Japan. It's a really big move for us!"

Per Diem—The pay a servicemember receives to cover the cost of travel while on temporary duty.

PLDC—*Primary Leadership Developmental Course.* For enlisted personnel.

POA—*Power of Attorney.* A legal document that allows you to conduct business on behalf of your servicemember in his absence. Don't let him leave home without giving you one!

POTUS—*President of the United States.* This term is reserved for a president you really hate, and it was often used for President Clinton, who was generally disliked by the military community. Most presidents are referred to as "Commander in Chief."

POV—*Personally Owned Vehicle.* Your car or truck.

PSD—*Personnel Support Detachment.* Consider it the company personnel department.

PT—*Physical Training.* Usually the morning exercises required by each command.

PX—*Post Exchange* (in Army terms). The department store on base. The Marines call it "MCX," the Air Force calls it "BX," and the Navy calls it "Exchange." If you're not confused already, it is also referred to as "AAFES" (pronounced "a-fees") because it is operated by the Army and Air Forces Exchange System.

QTRS—*Quarters.* Your living area, a.k.a house or apartment.

Rank—The title and level at which your servicemember has been promoted in the military hierarchy. For example, a Marine who passed boot camp has earned the title of Private and can later be promoted to Private First Class, then Lance Corporal, and so on. Rank is tied to pay grade, which determines your servicemember's level of Basic Pay.

REDUX—One of two types of pension plans for military retirees. The other type is High-3.

Relocation—To move your household to a new place.

RIF—*Reduction in Force.* Layoffs with honorable discharge. Not necessarily a bad thing if you get a good separation bonus.

SBP—*Survivor Benefit Plan.* The pittance you get as a widow if he dies.

SGLI—*Servicemembers' Group Life Insurance.* The inexpensive term life insurance plan provided by the Department of Defense.

Space A—*Space Available.* Refers to remaining seats on military transport planes that are available for servicemembers and families to travel for leisure or relocation.

TDY or TAD—*Temporary Duty/Temporary Assigned Duty.* Temporary assignment to a station or post, usually a training program. Spouse and family are typically not allowed to accompany a servicemember unless they pay for it out of their own pocket.

Threatcon—*Threat Condition.* The level of security on base that determines how much the gate guards will harass you. Threatcon Alpha means we are at war and you are not allowed on base unless you live there.

Tricare—The military's very own HMO.

TSP—*Thrift Savings Plan.* A retirement savings plan every service-member should participate in.

Unaccompanied Tour—A permanent duty station in which the servicemember's family is not allowed to relocate or live with the servicemember. These tours are usually in remote, difficult locations, such as Korea or islands in the Indian Ocean, and last for one year.

USA—*United States Army.* Gotcha! You'd think they'd find a different acronym.

XO—*Executive Officer.* Second in command to the Commanding Officer (CO) and usually the bad guy of the unit.

ACKNOWLEDGMENTS

I would like to express to the world how truly blessed I am to be married to my husband, Fernando. I completed this book just before giving birth to our son, Alejandro. Five weeks and three sets of grandparents later, Fernando watched Alejandro full-time while I banged out edits for an early pub date. He has supported me in every aspect of my career, attentively sharing in my hopes, fears, and endless strategizing. I can't thank him enough for being my partner in life.

I would also like to thank the amazing Advisory Board of *CinC*House.com for sharing a vision of the military community and then actually making it happen. In particular, Sandy Aldridge, my "XO" and director of Operation Homefront, and Meri Rettinger, our events guru and budding TV star, stand out for their formidable effort and sheer dedication. Tammy Sikes buttresses them, working ten-plus hours a day helping military families in Southern California. Jennifer Scales has started the rallying cry to support our deployed troops at home, and is always there to help a fellow girlfriend. Robyne Ruterbusch and Jennifer Morrow have spent endless hours with their fingers in the wind, attuned to change, and then counseling on new directions. Finally, Marsha Butler has generously lent her weight and credibility to *CinC*House as a senior military family leader. She and Jennifer Morrow have also served as excellent editors and journalistic *compadres*. All of these women have been a wonderful source of encouragement for this book while also helping me free up time to write.

Additionally, my girlfriends MaryAnn, Dorothy, Dawna, Michelle, Belle, Rose, Kay Ann, and many others deserve credit for lending me their tales of military life—as well as the personal inspiration that went with them. Linda Blanz of the Navy–Marine Corps Relief Society also deserves credit for reviewing the financial portions of this book and teaching me everything I know about military pay.

Finally, I would like to thank my agent, Kristen Auclair, and my editor, Marcela Landres, for taking a chance on me and the community of military wives and women. Your encouragement and support have meant more to all of us than you know.

INDEX